Assessing and Teaching Reading Comprehension and Pre-Writing, 3–5

Volume 3

K. Michael Hibbard
Elizabeth A. Wagner

EYE ON EDUCATION
6 DEPOT WAY WEST, SUITE 106
LARCHMONT, NY 10538
(914) 833–0551
(914) 833–0761 fax
www.eyeoneducation.com

Library of Congress Cataloging-in-Publication Data

HIbbard, K. Michael.
    Assessing and teaching reading comprehension and pre-writing, grades 3-5 / K. Michael Hibbard and Elizabeth A. Wagner.
        p. cm.
    "Volume 3."
    Includes bibliographical references.
    ISBN 1-930556-54-3
    1. Language arts (Elementary) 2. Reading comprehension--Ability testing. I. Wagner, Elizabeth A., 1950- II. Title.

LB1576.H3447 2003
372.6--dc21

                                        2003040795
10 9 8 7 6 5 4 3 2 1

Editorial and production services provided by
Richard H. Adin Freelance Editorial Services
52 Oakwood Blvd., Poughkeepsie, NY 12603-4112
(914-471-3566)

Also Available from EYE ON EDUCATION

**Assessing and Teaching Reading Comprehension
and Pre-Writing, K-3, Volume 1**
K. Michael Hibbard and Elizabeth A. Wagner

**Assessing and Teaching Reading Comprehension
and Writing, K-3, Volume 2**
K. Michael Hibbard and Elizabeth A. Wagner

**Assessing and Teaching Reading Comprehension
and Writing, 3-5, Volume 4**
K. Michael Hibbard and Elizabeth A. Wagner

**Differentiated Instruction:
A Guide for Elementary School Teachers**
Amy Benjamin

**Reading, Writing, and Gender:
Instructional Strategies and Classroom Activities That
Work for Girls and Boys**
Gail Goldberg and Barbara Roswell

**Teaching, Learning, and Assessment Together:
The Reflective Classroom**
Arthur K. Ellis

**Buddies:
Reading, Writing, and Math Lessons**
Pia Hansen Powell

**Mathematics the Write Way:
Activities for Every Elementary Classroom**
Marilyn Neil

**Better Instruction Through Assessment:
What Your Student Are Trying to Tell You**
Leslie Walker Wilson

Assessment Portfolios for Elementary Students
Milwaukee Public Schools

**Beyond Stories:
Young Children's Nonfiction Composition**
Susan Britsch

Table of Contents

1

A Roadmap to This Book

Objectives for This Chapter

♦ An overview of this book.
♦ Connections between the Standards for the Assessment of Reading and Writing by the National Council of Teachers of English and the International Reading Association, and the strategies presented in this book.

Reading is a complex behavior including decoding words, developing fluency, and improving comprehension. This book focuses on strategies to teach and assess reading comprehension. The reading comprehension/thinking skill framework used throughout this book is based on the approach to reading comprehension developed by the National Assessment of Educational Progress (NAEP). The materials and strategies presented here support the national English Language Arts Standards and will help teachers and administrators address the challenges of the No Child Left Behind legislation.

A Graphic Overview of This Book

Figure 1.1 presents a graphic that highlights the contents of this book. Students use higher-order thinking skills and reading comprehension strategies to interact with texts, and to connect those texts to other texts and to personal experiences. They reveal their comprehension through speaking, drawing, graphic organizers, and writing. This book focuses on the pre-writing activities of speaking, drawing, and graphic organizers. The second book in this series *Assessing and Teaching Reading Comprehension and Writing Grades 3–5* (Vol. 4), focuses on using these pre-writing activities to support narrative (telling a story), expository (explaining, informing, or teaching), and persuasive writing.

Authentic performance tasks are created to engage students with fiction and nonfiction texts and use thinking skills such as sequencing, listing, describing, categorizing, inferring, predicting, comparing, contrasting, judging, and evaluating. The performance tasks ask the students to discuss what they have learned; draw and label pictures, and put information into a wide range of graphic organizers.

Assessment tools including assessment lists, analytic rubrics, and holistic rubrics are used to assess and evaluate this type of student work.

Figure 1.1 shows that following classroom routines, following directions, working cooperatively with others, and self-assessment creates a foundation for the improvement of language arts skills. Self-assessment is an essential part of the strategies presented in this book and is introduced through helping students improve their behavior in the classroom.

The Topics for Each Chapter

Figure 1.2 presents the topics for each chapter.

Figure 1.1. Revealing Reading Comprehension through Speaking, Drawing, Graphic Organizers and Writing

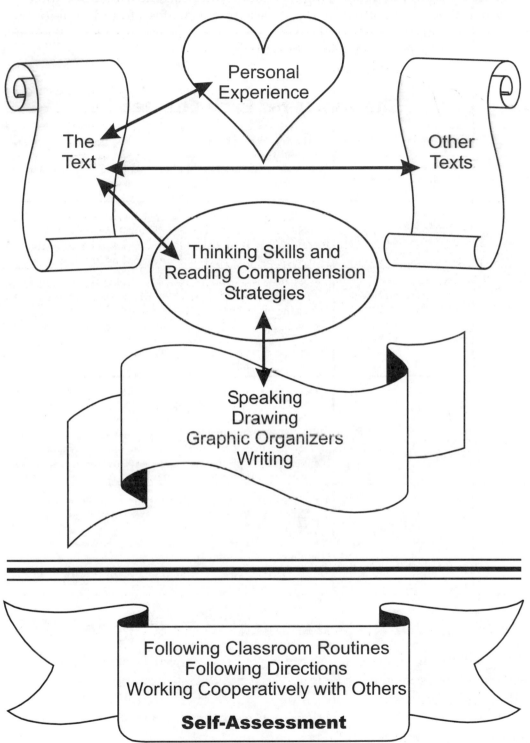

Figure 1.2. Topics for Each Chapter

Chapter Number	Chapter Title	Topics
1	A Roadmap to This Book	• An overview of this book. • Explanation of how the Standards for the Assessment of Reading and Writing by the National Council of Teachers of English and the International Reading Association are carried out by the strategies presented in this book.
2	Assessing Classroom Behavior, Work Habits, and Cooperative Group Learning Skills As an Introduction to Self-Assessment	• Strategies to engage students in learning about the specific behaviors they should exhibit in the classroom. • Strategies to engage students in self-assessment so they learn to take more responsibility for their performance and improve their behavior and academic performance.
3	A Framework for Reading Comprehension	• The reading comprehension framework from the National Assessment of Educational Progress (NAEP). • Using the reading comprehension framework to create comprehension questions for fiction and nonfiction.
4	Assessing Comprehension of Fiction through Drawing	• Strategies for using a framework for reading comprehension that focuses on thinking-skill verbs to make performance tasks for fiction, asking students to draw and present orally. • Strategies to make analytic rubrics and assessment lists for judging the quality of drawings and oral presentations. • Strategies to use performance tasks and assessment tools in the context of language arts lessons.
5	Assessing Comprehension of Nonfiction through Drawing	• Strategies for using a framework for reading comprehension that focuses on thinking-skill verbs to make performance tasks for nonfiction, asking students to draw and present orally. • Strategies to make analytic rubrics and assessment lists for judging the quality of drawings and oral presentations. • Strategies to use performance tasks and assessment tools in the context of language arts lessons.
6	Assessing Comprehension through the Use of Graphic Organizers	• Strategies for using graphic organizers to help students process information according to the thinking-skill verb used in the task. • Strategies to create performance tasks that use graphic organizers and oral presentation. • Strategies to create assessment tools to assess the quality of a student's use of graphic organizers.

Standards for the Assessment of Reading and Writing

The following pages are a summary of the standards from the book, *Standards for the Assessment of Reading and Writing*, 1994, International Reading Association and the National Council of Teachers of English, ISBN 0-87207-674-1. The description of the connections between the standards, and the materials and strategies presented in this book follow.

Standard 1: The Interests of the Student Are Paramount in Assessment

Summary of Standard 1	*Connection between the Standard and the Materials and Strategies of This Book*
The purpose of assessment is to improve student performance. The very process of assessing reading comprehension and writing should make the student a better reader and writer. Reading and writing are used to find and communicate information, ideas, and feelings. Assessment should be authentic and focus on how well students use reading and writing to learn and communicate. Finally, because the assessment process includes opportunities for the student to assess and evaluate the quality of their work, the assessment process helps the student become a reflective learner.	The performance tasks presented in this book are authentic opportunities for students to use reading and writing for learning and communication. Each performance task is built around thinking-skill verbs and components of the writing process. The assessment lists are derived from rubrics related to speaking, drawing, using graphic organizers, and writing. The performance tasks are embedded in units of instruction to serve as learning activities and opportunities to assess student performance. Each performance task has an assessment list that is used before, during, and after a task is completed to assess the quality of a student's work.

Standard 2: The Primary Purpose of Assessment Is to Improve Teaching and Learning

Summary of Standard 2	*Connection between the Standard and the Materials and Strategies of This Book*
The interests of the student are served if teaching and learning improves. This standard emphasizes the importance of reflection by both the student and the teacher. Through self-reflection, the learner identifies strengths and weaknesses and then sets and carries out goals to improve their own performance. Likewise, through self-reflection, the teacher identifies strengths and weaknesses of the materials and strategies of teaching and works to improve both. The assessment process must foster this self-reflection and improvement on the part of both student and teacher.	Self-assessment helps students learn to pay attention and take responsibility for the quality of their work. Analytic and holistic rubrics for drawing, speaking, and using graphic organizers are found in volume one of this two-set series, *Assessing and Teaching Reading Comprehension and Pre-Writing K–3.* Analytic and holistic rubrics for various types of writing are found in this book. These assessment tools provide a source of information for teachers to use to gain information about student performance. Teachers assess the students' work and the quality of their self-assessment through the use of assessment lists and rubrics. The information from using assessment lists and rubrics becomes the basis for plans to improve instruction.

Standard 3: Assessment Must Reflect and Enable Critical Inquiry into Curriculum and Instruction

Summary of Standard 3	Connection between the Standard and the Materials and Strategies of This Book
Because reading and writing are complex acts used in very flexible ways, curriculum should plan for the use of reading and writing for these authentic purposes. The curriculum must also include assessments that are well-suited to authentic purposes of reading and writing. Analysis and reflection on the data from assessments helps the teacher decide if the curriculum and assessments are encouraging the use of reading and writing as authentic tools for learning.	Each performance task is an authentic use of reading and writing for the purposes of learning and communicating. Each performance task asks the student to produce a product for a specific audience. Students are learning that reading and writing serves to answer their own questions and also to teach, inform, or entertain an audience. Teachers evaluate the success of performance tasks as authentic opportunities to use reading and writing.

Standard 4: Assessment Must Recognize and Reflect the Intellectually and Socially Complex Nature of Reading and Writing and the Important Roles of School, Home, and Society in Literacy Development

Summary of Standard 4	Connection between the Standard and the Materials and Strategies of This Book
Reading and writing are such complex acts that no one type of assessment is sufficient. Therefore, a set of carefully chosen assessments should be used. These assessments must include opportunities for students to show how well they can use reading and writing for authentic learning and communication. In addition, data from these assessments should not be reduced to a single rating or score.	Performance tasks should be one component in a balanced literacy assessment plan. Teachers and administrators should work together to use a set of assessments that helps the classroom teacher make decisions to improve instruction. The assessment lists and analytic rubrics used in this book provide information about the specific strengths and weaknesses of each student.

Standard 5: Assessment Must Be Fair and Equitable

Summary of Standard 5	Connection between the Standard and the Materials and Strategies of This Book
Assessments must be free of cultural bias and students must have a reasonable opportunity to learn what is to be assessed.	Performance tasks and assessment tools are created and modified by teachers to be fair and equitable to students. Teachers select a performance task to use and then plan instruction to help students learn what the performance task will ask them to do. Therefore the students will have many opportunities to learn the content of what will be assessed.

Standard 6: The Consequences of an Assessment Procedure Are the First, and the Most Important, Consideration in Establishing the Validity of the Assessment

Summary of Standard 6	Connection between the Standard and the Materials and Strategies of This Book
Assessment must help to improve student performance in the authentic use of reading and writing for learning and communication. A set of assessments would include both tests for specific skills and assessments of how well students read and write to learn and communicate. Including performance assessments in the assessment plan will encourage teachers to use reading and writing in the classroom for authentic purposes. Assessments should help classroom teachers make day-to-day decisions that help adjust and differentiate their materials and strategies to improve the performance of all students. The amount of time spent in assessment must be balanced with the time spent using data from assessment to teach and learn.	Performance tasks and assessment tools are one component of instruction in balance with other classroom activities. The assessment lists provide an efficient way for the teacher to communicate expectations to students and to assess their performance. The performance tasks are worth the time they take. Performance tasks ask students to use knowledge and language arts skills in the context of constructing thoughts and communicating them to others. Classroom instruction that precedes the performance tasks focus both on specific skills and how to use them to solve real learning and communications problems.

Standard 7: The Teacher Is the Most Important Agent of Assessment

Summary of Standard 7	Connection between the Standard and the Materials and Strategies of This Book
First and foremost, teachers should be readers and writers. They should continuously improve their knowledge of the research and best practices of reading and writing. Some of the best professional development occurs when teachers discuss and share judgments about student work and plan materials and strategies to improve student performance.	Conversations about student work, as discussed through the lens of assessment lists and rubrics is excellent professional development. Based on what they learn, teachers plan improvements in performance tasks and their supporting materials. Learning to modify existing performance tasks and assessment lists, and to collaborate in designing new tasks, help teachers learn more about the content and process skills in their disciplines.

Standard 8: The Assessment Process Should Involve Multiple Perspectives and Sources of Data

Summary of Standard 5	Connection between the Standard and the Materials and Strategies of This Book
A variety of assessments must be used to take a comprehensive look at student performance. Anecdotal Records, Running Records with Retelling, High Frequency Words, Letter Name Inventory, Letter Sound Inventory, Developmental Spelling, Dictation, the Gates MacGinitie Reading Test, and Performance Tasks as presented in this book are examples of assessment to consider. There should be a balance between assessment of skill and assessments of authentic use of reading and writing for learning and communication.	Performance tasks are only one component of a balanced assessment plan that includes other tests, such as running records, retelling, and teacher observations.

Standard 9: Assessment Must Be Based in the School Community

Summary of Standard 9	Connection between the Standard and the Materials and Strategies of This Book
It is important for educators, parents, and other members of the community to talk with one another to understand and communicate how reading and writing are rich, complex, flexible tools people use to learn and communicate. The school's curriculum, instructional practices, and assessments all work together to reflect an understanding of reading and writing. This common understanding will help a partnership flourish among educators, parents, and other community members.	Performance tasks and assessment lists are excellent ways to show parents how reading and writing are tools for learning. Student work accompanied by an assessment list that has been used by the student, and by the teacher to assess the quality of the self-assessment and the student work is valued by parents. Performance tasks, assessment lists, and student work are excellent materials for parent conferences.

Standard 10: All Members of the Educational Community—Students, Parents, Teachers, Administrators, Policy Makers, and the Public—Must Have a Voice in the Development, Interpretation, and Reporting of Assessment

Summary of Standard 10	Connection between the Standard and the Materials and Strategies of This Book
Educators, parents, and other members of the educational community engage in a dialogue that reflects and defines the understanding of how the data will be communicated to the public. The outcome of this process is that parents are well-informed about their children's performance in reading and writing and are happy with the work that teachers are doing to improve performance.	The use of performance tasks and assessment lists as one component of teaching and assessment must be explained to the Board of Education, parents, and others. The authentic nature of performance tasks makes them very appealing to all concerned audiences. It is important to show how data on student performance is generated from performance tasks and how it is used to drive instruction. Finally, it is important to show improvements in student performance over time.

Standard 11: Parents Must Be Involved As Active, Essential Participants in the Assessment Process

Summary of Standard 11	*Connection between the Standard and the Materials and Strategies of This Book*
Schools need to reach out to parents in a wide variety of ways that respond to the diverse needs and life commitments of the families. Reporting procedures such as report cards, parent conferences, portfolios, and letters from the school accompanying state test data reports should be planned in collaboration with parents. Parents should also be encouraged to participate in professional development offerings.	Performance tasks and student work can become a central part of parent conferences, portfolio exhibitions, and other parent meetings. Performance tasks and assessment lists are easy ways to teach parents about what is important in teaching and learning.

2

Teaching and Assessing Classroom Behavior, Work Habits, and Cooperative Groups As an Introduction to Self-Assessment

Topics in This Chapter

♦ Strategies to engage students in learning the specific behaviors they should exhibit in the classroom.

♦ Strategies to engage students in self-assessment so that they learn to take more responsibility for their behavior and academic performance.

Note: A glossary of terms is at the end of the chapter.

Begin the Acts of Self-Reflection and Self-Regulation through Focusing on Student Behaviors in the Classroom

Classroom management is an important foundation for learning activities throughout the year. Carrying out classroom routines; working with partners, small groups, and the class as a whole group; and students' personal work habits and study skills are challenges for the teacher as well as the students. When these behaviors are constructive, lessons run more smoothly. But when these behaviors are below standard, teaching and learning are both compromised.

Performance assessment is easily introduced in the context of specific behaviors that are important to a smoothly running classroom, productive group work, and effective personal work habits. Because these behaviors occur every day, the students have concrete experience with them. Student performance in these areas can usually be improved through the strategies of self-assessment and self-regulation. Students can experience success and learn to value the use of assessment lists and the strategies of performance-based learning and assessment.

This chapter shows how to use performance-based learning and assessment to improve classroom management and student behavior. This work should be done at the beginning of the school year to foster independence on the part of students so the teacher can focus more time on academics.

A Sequence of Steps to Use Performance Assessment to Improve Student Performance

The following list presents one sequence of steps a teacher could use to improve student performance:

♦ Select a type of behavior, skill, or work to assess and improve.
♦ Identify the specifics of that type of behavior, skill, or work.
♦ Create an analytic rubric to further describe the behavior, skill, or work.
♦ Create an assessment list to focus students' attention on the details of their behavior and work.
♦ Collect models or examples of actual student performance and work that show the level of performance expected from them.
♦ Teach students skills and behaviors.
♦ Teach students to use assessment lists.
♦ Teach students to use models of excellent work as targets or goals.
♦ Teach students to set goals to improve their own performance.
♦ Repeat these steps.

Skills and Behaviors to Pay Attention To

1. Classroom Skills to Assess, including:
♦ Following routines
♦ Showing respect and courtesy to:
  • classmates
  • the teacher
  • visitors
  • substitute teachers

- the classroom and its contents

2. Study Skills and Work Habits, Including:
  - Coming to class prepared
  - Managing time
  - Organizing notes, notebooks, and other information
  - Getting homework done

3. Group Learning Skills Include:
  - Listening
  - Taking turns
  - Contributing
  - Encouraging the participation of others
  - Checking for understanding
  - Checking directions
  - Getting work done on time
  - Managing materials and cleaning up

Use "T" Charts to Identify Specific, Observable Behaviors to Assess

A "T" Chart is a type of graphic organizer designed to help identify specific, observable behaviors that are related to a general behavior such as showing respect and courtesy, managing time, or encouraging a friend to participate in a group project.

The three "T" Charts in this chapter show the final products of classroom discussions held by the teacher with students. Figures 2.1, 2.2, and 2.3 show "T" Charts resulting from classroom discussions about the behaviors listed on the top of each. Each "T" Chart may take several discussions over a few days to complete. *The words in italics* are what the teacher scribed onto the chart from discussions with students.

After the teacher talks about the general behavior or skill, such as managing time, he asks the students to imagine what it would "look like" if a student managed time well. Students take turns suggesting "looks like" statements. The teacher asks follow-up questions to focus these "looks like" statements. For example, a student may say, "I get the project done by the time it should be turned in." The teacher may ask, "What does it look like when you are working to get the project done by the time it should be turned in? What are you doing that tells me that you are working to get the project done by the time it should be turned in?" The student may reply, "I look at the clock to check how much time I have left, and I get my project done and turned in when the time is up." That specific, observable behavior is written in the "looks like" column of the "T" Chart.

After a few items are written in the "looks like" column, the teacher and students then turn their attention to the "sounds like" column of the "T" chart and continue the discussion. During the first session, the class may only find a few items for each column. It may take more experience with, and thinking about, following classroom routines to add more items to the "T" Chart. Completed "T" Charts can be displayed in the classroom.

Note: The "T" Chart in Figure 2.2 shows the items selected to be Sure Things, "ST," and the item selected to be a Challenge, "C." The assessment list in Figure 2.8 was constructed based on the use of the "T" Chart in Figure 2.2.

Figure 2.1. Behaviors that Show Respect and Courtesy

When I show respect and courtesy

it looks like:	*it sounds like:*
My lips are not moving when someone else is speaking.	I am silent when someone else is speaking.
I am looking at the person who is speaking.	I say please and thank you.
I raise my hand when I want to speak.	I say good morning to the teacher or the substitute teacher.
I share my materials with my classmates.	When a substitute asks a question, I give a clear answer.
I do not grab things from my classmates.	I ask permission to go to another center in the classroom.
I do not crowd in front of others in line.	I never use put-downs.
I keep my hands to myself.	I never call a person names.
I clean up my workspace.	I may disagree, but I do not argue.
If I see a piece of trash on the floor, I throw it away.	I do not sound angry.
I do not make marks on my desk.	I ask permission before I use something that belongs to someone else.
I put things I have used back in the correct place.	I ask a classmate if he needs help if it looks like he needs help.
I put permission slips, notes, homework, and other things in the correct box on the teacher's desk.	I use people's names when I speak to them.
I smile at classmates and other people in the classroom.	I motion with my hand to invite a classmate to work with me or be in my group.

"Sure Thing" and "Challenge" Items

Figure 2.2 presents a "T" Chart for Managing Time Well. The teacher has marked three of the items "ST" to show that the students are so good at using these particular behaviors that they are "Sure Things." For example, the children in this teacher's class are very good about reading the assessment list before they begin their performance task and using the assessment list at the end to check their work.

Two items in Figure 2.2 are marked with a "C" to indicate that the students do not yet do a good job with these behaviors, i.e., the behavior is a "Challenge" to them. For example, the children in this class are not yet good about making a plan of what they need to do and writing it in their assignment book.

Figure 2.2. Managing Time Well

When I manage my time well

	it looks like:		*it sounds like:*
	I get to school on time.		I am not talking to my friends when I should be getting to class on time.
	I get to my classroom on time.		I ask when the project is due.
C	I make a plan of what I need to do, and I write it in my assignment book.		I ask for help if I am not sure what to put in my assignment book.
ST	I collect all the things I will need to use before I start my work.	ST	I am not talking to my friends when I should be doing my own work.
	I read all the directions at the beginning of a project.		I, for example, would say, "ten minutes left" if I am working with a partner.
ST	I read the assessment list for my work before I begin the performance task, and I use the assessment list at the end to check my work.	C	If I am having a problem getting the work done on time, I would talk to the teacher about it.
	I look at the clock to check how much time I have left, and I get my project done and turned in when the time is up.		
	I am not talking to anyone else when I am doing my own work.		
	I raise my hand when I have a question to a problem that I cannot figure out.		

Key:

ST   = **Sure Thing**, e.g, what students already do well

C   = **Challenge**, e.g, what students need to improve

Figure 2.3. Encouraging a Friend to Participate

When I encourage a friend to participate

it looks like:	*it sounds like:*
I look at the person in my group who is speaking.	I say hello to everyone in the group.
I smile at all the people in my group.	I use the person's name when I speak to someone in my group.
My body is leaning towards the group to show that I am interested.	I use my "good manners" by saying please and thank you.
My mouth is not moving when my friend is sharing.	When I see that a person is not getting a turn, I say, for example, "Bill, what do you think?"
After my friends stops talking, it looks like I am asking him a question.	When someone is speaking, I am quiet.
If a person in my group is not speaking, I turn to that person, and it looks like I am asking him a question.	When the person is done speaking, I ask a question that shows that I was paying attention to what he was saying.
After I ask the person who has not spoken a question, it looks like he begins to speak.	
When I listen to the person speaking, it looks like I am interested in what he has to say.	

Creating Analytic Rubrics

Working on a "T" Chart helps the teacher think about the details of specific behaviors or skills important to a more general behavior. Those details are captured in the "T" Chart. An analytic rubric based on a "T Chart" can be created. Figures 2.4, 2.5, and 2.6 (pages 21, 22, and 23) show analytic rubrics for the three corresponding "T" Charts in Figures 2.1, 2.3, and 2.4.

To create the analytic rubric for managing time, the teacher makes a list of the types of behaviors or skills important to managing time. Then the teacher puts those statements into the left column of the analytic rubric, labeled "Specific Behavior."

Next, the teacher writes specific descriptions for each of the three levels of performance relevant to that behavior. The teacher describes what it is like when a student is "Terrific" at managing time, what a student is like when he or she is only "Okay" at managing time, and what behavior that "Needs Work" is like. Note that the title for the lowest category of performance is not a negative statement such as "Poor Performance." It is stated as "Needs Work" and means "this behavior needs work and we can do it."

Note that each specific behavior in each rubric has the "weight of 1." This means that the teacher has decided that all the specific behaviors are of equal importance.

Some rubrics in subsequent chapters show that some items of analytic rubrics are more important than other items and, thus, have more "weight," e.g., worth more points.

Each of the three levels of performance is weighted. "Terrific" has a weight of 3, "Okay" has a weight of 2, and "Needs Work" has a weight of 1. The score for being a "Terrific" listener when someone else is talking is 1x3=3.

Using Analytic Rubrics

Analytic rubrics are tools that teachers make and use themselves. Sometimes, teachers at the same or similar grade levels collaborate to create a rubric so that they all have a common understanding of the levels of quality of the specific behaviors important to a general behavior, such as following classroom routines.

An individual teacher or a team can use the analytic rubric to identify the strengths and needs of students and then plan to adjust and differentiate instruction to improve student performance. Using the same analytic rubric over the course of the year, or several years, helps the teacher or team see and describe "progress over time" in student behavior. This kind of data can be useful in setting classroom or school improvement objectives and in assessing the degree to which the objectives are met.

Students in the upper elementary grades see the whole analytic rubric and learn about it one behavior at a time. The teacher may present one specific behavior, such as "Keeping An Assignment Book and Calendar to Manage Time" and the descriptions of the three levels of performance—Terrific, Okay, and Needs Work. The students may then talk about their behavior and decide what their performance has been like. If their behavior is less than "Terrific," they can set goals and plan to improve.

"Sure Thing" and "Challenge" Items

Figure 2.5 (page 22) presents an analytic rubric for Managing Time and it shows that three specific behaviors have been marked "ST" to indicate that the children in this class are consistently exhibiting this behavior so that it is a "Sure Thing." Two specific behaviors have been marked "C" to indicate that the children are not yet good at these behaviors, and, therefore, these behaviors are currently "Challenge" behaviors.

Figure 2.4. Analytic Rubric for Showing Respect and Courtesy

Specific Behavior	Levels of Performance		
	Terrific Weight = 3	Okay Weight = 2	Needs Work Weight = 1
Listening When Someone Else Is Speaking Weight = 1	I always look at the speaker and do not talk when another person is talking. I always raise my hand when I want to speak.	I usually look at the speaker and do not talk when another person is talking. I usually raise my hand when I want to speak.	I look away from the speaker and talk when someone else is speaking. I need to remember to raise my hand when I want to speak.
Using Polite Language Weight = 1	I always say please, thank you, and good morning.	I usually say please, thank you, and good morning.	I often forget to say please, thank you, and good morning.
Taking Turns Weight = 1	I always wait my turn.	I usually wait my turn.	I interrupt too much and do not wait for my turn.
Avoiding Put-Downs and Name Calling Weight = 1	I never use put-downs or names about other people, even when they are not around.	Sometimes I forget and use a put-down, but I catch myself and stop.	Sometimes I forget and use put-downs or names. I am not catching myself quickly enough.
Using Materials and Supplies Weight = 1	I am careful to not waste materials and supplies. I share with others.	I sometimes catch myself using too much.	I need to work on not wasting supplies so that others will have enough.
Keeping the Room Neat and Clean Weight = 1	I keep my own work area clean and organized. I clean up other places in the room where I have worked.	I usually keep my own work area clean and organized. I usually clean up other places in the room where I have worked.	My own work area is not clean or organized and I forget to clean up the other areas of the room in which I work.

Figure 2.5. Analytic Rubric for Managing Time

Specific Behavior	Levels of Performance		
	Terrific Weight = 3	Okay Weight = 2	Needs Work Weight = 1
Being on Time Weight = 1	I am always on time for school and class.	I am almost always on time for school and class.	I am late for school or class too often.
Keeping an Assignment Book Weight = 1 *C*	My assignment book has a calendar and I mark it to show when each assignment is due. I keep the directions for my assignments in my notebook until the work is complete.	My assignment book has a calendar, and I usually mark it to show when each assignment is due. I usually keep the directions for my assignments in my notebook until the work is complete	I do not keep my assignment book or calendar up to date. Sometimes I lose the directions for my assignments.
Being Prepared to Do Work Weight = 1 *ST*	I am always prepared with all the materials and supplies I need to do my work.	I am usually prepared with all the materials and supplies I need to do my work.	I am not prepared to begin my work.
Following Directions and Using Assessment Lists Weight = 1 *ST*	I read the directions carefully and study the assessment list to know what I have to do. I use the assessment list to assess my own work.	I usually read the directions carefully and usually study the assessment list to know what I have to do. I usually use the assessment list to assess my own work.	Sometimes, I skip reading the directions and just start my work. I do not use the assessment list.
Asking for Help Weight = 1 *C*	If I have a question, I try to figure out the answer before I ask for help.	If I have a question, I usually try to figure out the answer before I ask for help.	If I have a question, I ask for help before I have tried to figure out the answer.
Doing My Own Work Weight = 1 *ST*	I work quietly when I am working alone.	I usually work quietly.	I talk too much when I should be working quietly.
Keeping Track of Time Weight = 1	I always know how much time is left before my work is due.	I usually know how much time is left before my work is due.	I often lose track of time and I am surprised when the time is up.
Getting Work Done on Time Weight = 1	I always get my work done on time.	I usually get my work done on time.	My work is often late.

Figure 2.6. Analytic Rubric for Encouraging a Friend to Participate

Specific Behavior	*Levels of Performance*		
	Terrific Weight = 3	**Okay** Weight = 2	**Needs Work** Weight = 1
Asks the friend to participate. Weight = 1	Often the student says things like, "What do you think about _____?", "Can you draw the _____?", "Would you please make the _____?". Each question is specific to the task at hand.	Sometimes the students ask questions pertinent to the task to engage other students.	The student seldom asks questions.
Listens actively. Weight = 1	Always looks at the speaker and does not talk when someone else is talking.	Usually looks at the speaker and does not talk when someone else is talking.	Often does not look at the speaker. Often talks when someone else is talking.
Is courteous and polite. Weight = 1	Always says "please" and "thank you" and uses other polite language. Never uses impolite language.	Often says "please" and "thank you" and uses other polite language. Never uses impolite language.	Usually does not say "please" and "thank you," and usually does not use other polite language. The student may also use impolite language.
Acts friendly. Weight = 1	Smiles when appropriate and is always kind.	Smiles when appropriate and is usually kind.	Usually does not smile and is seldom kind. May be unkind.
Keeps hands and feet to self. Weight = 1	Always keeps hands and feet to self.	Usually keeps hands and feet to self.	Often is inappropriate in the use of hands and feet.

Creating Assessment Lists from Analytic Rubrics and T Charts

Strategy of Creating Assessment Lists

The assessment list is a tool to help students pay attention to classroom behaviors, skills, and class work. It contains items that are relevant to the general skill, behavior, or work being assessed, and has a reasonable number of items that students will be able to pay attention to. In the beginning, an assessment list may only contain three or four items because the students are ready to pay attention to only a few things. When the students are comfortable with short assessment lists, then the teacher adds one or two more items. Assessment lists are usually never more than one page long and usually contain no more than eight to ten items.

On a six-item assessment list, three or four of the items describe specific skills or behaviors that are "sure things," i.e., behaviors or skills with which the students are comfortable and that the students perform at the "Terrific" or "Okay" level. Paying attention to these behaviors or skills is encouraging to the students and reinforces positive behavior.

One or two items on the assessment list is a "challenge" because most of the students are performing at the "Needs Work" level. By placing a "challenge" item on the assessment list, the teacher has selected a focus for instruction and improvement in student performance. Classroom time will be devoted to discussions, demonstrations, modeling, and practice of this skill or behavior.

The "T" Chart shown in Figure 2.2 is about managing time. Three items in the "T" Chart are marked "ST" and two are marked "C" by a teacher who used the "T" Chart to assess the overall strengths and needs of her students before she created the assessment list in Figure 2.8.

That same teacher could have used the analytic rubric in Figure 2.5, and in preparation for creating the assessment list, could have circled the levels of behavior of her students relevant to following classroom routines. Then, that information could have been used to create the assessment list in Figure 2.8.

When students are familiar with assessment lists, involve them in reviewing the "T" Charts and helping to create assessment lists with "sure things" and "challenges."

Summary of the Steps in Creating an Assessment List

♦ Select a general behavior or work habit to assess.

♦ Use a "T" Chart or an Analytic Rubric to describe the specific skills or specific observable behaviors relevant to the general behavior or work habit.

- Select three or four specific skills or observable behaviors on which the students do very well. These will be the "Sure Thing" items on the assessment list. Select one or two specific skills or observable behaviors on which the students do poorly. These will be the "Challenge" items on the assessment list.
- Write the items on the assessment list in an order that places the "Challenge" items in the middle of the list.
- Write the items on the assessment list in the form of questions that the student will ask himself during self-assessment.
- Assure that the items are stated in student language and are short and to the point.
- Assign points to each item in the assessment list.
- Never make more than one page of assessment list items. Use four or five items in the beginning and eight to ten items when students are experienced and comfortable with using assessment lists.

Formats for Assessment Lists

Figures 2.7, 2.8, and 2.9 show a format for assessment lists. Here the assessment list is on one piece of paper that can be used by individual or small groups of students.

The items of the behavior or work to be assessed are listed down the left-hand column. The points possible, i.e., points assigned to this item, are shown so the student knows how important each item is.

Other formats for assessment lists include:

- Large wall posters
- Sentence strip holders with one item on each strip
- Activity center posters
- Small, individual assessment lists taped to the student's desk or in their homework folder or journal.

Assigning Points to Items in Assessment Lists

The analytic rubrics in Figures 2.4, 2.5, and 2.6 show three levels of quality for each specific behavior in the rubrics. One way to assign points is to give three (3) points for "Terrific," two points (2) for "Okay," and one (1) point for "Needs Work."

All the specific behaviors in each of the three analytic rubrics in this chapter are of equal weight. Each has been assigned the "weight" of "1."

Figure 2.10 (page 29) shows how points are assigned to each cell in the analytic rubric.

Figure 2.7. Performance Task Assessment List: Showing Respect and Courtesy

		Points Earned	
Item	*Assessment Points Possible*	*Assessed by Self*	*Assessed by Teacher*
1. Did I listen to the speaker who brought the hawks and owls to our classroom?	3	_____	_____
2. Did I say thank you to the speaker?	3	_____	_____
3. Did I wait patiently for my turn to touch the skeleton of the hawk?	3	_____	_____
4. Was I very careful not to use any put-downs or call anyone names who did not want to touch the birds and skeletons?	3	_____	_____
5. Did I help straighten up the room after the science lesson?	3	_____	_____
Total	**15**	_____	_____

Terrific = 3   Okay = 2   Needs Work = 1

Figure 2.8. Performance Task Assessment List: Managing Time

Item	Assessment Points Possible	Points Earned	
		Assessed by Self	Assessed by Teacher
1. Did I have all of my supplies to complete my math work each day during the graphing project?	3	_____	_____
2. Did I follow directions for the graphing project and use the assessment accurately?	3	_____	_____
3. Did I use my assignment book and calendar to keep track of when my graphing project was due?	3	_____	_____
4. Did I complete my own work quietly when I was working at my desk and the teacher was working with a group or another student?	3	_____	_____
5. Did I ask for help when I needed it and after I had tried to answer the question myself?	3	_____	_____
Total	**15**	_____	_____

Terrific = 3   Okay = 2   Needs Work = 1

Figure 2.9. Performance Task Assessment List: Encouraging Others to Participate in Cooperative Group Activities

Item	Assessment Points Possible	Points Earned	
		Assessed by Self	Assessed by Teacher
1. During our book discussion, did I ask at least two other people in the group what they thought?	3	_____	_____
2. Did I listen to what each person said without interrupting or talking?	3	_____	_____
3. When I saw that a person in the group was not getting a turn, did I say something like, "It's Bill's turn now. What do you think Bill?"	3	_____	_____
4. Did I say kind things like, "That is a good idea!"?	3	_____	_____
5. Did I stay in my seat and keep my hands and feet to myself?	3	_____	_____
Total	15	_____	_____

Terrific = 3   Okay = 2   Needs Work = 1

Figure 2.10. Analytic Rubric for Managing Time

Each Specific Behavior Has the Weight of "1"			
Specific Behavior	Levels of Performance		
	Terrific Weight = 3	Okay Weight = 2	Needs Work Weight = 1
Being on Time Weight = 1	1x3 = 3	1x2 = 2	1x1 = 1
Keeping an Assignment Book Weight = 1	1x3 = 3	1x2 = 2	1x1 = 1
Being Prepared to Do Work Weight = 1	1x3 = 3	1x2 = 2	1x1 = 1
Following Directions and Using Assessment Lists Weight = 1	1x3 = 3	1x2 = 2	1x1 = 1
Asking for Help Weight = 1	1x3 = 3	1x2 = 2	1x1 = 1
Doing My Own Work Weight = 1	1x3 = 3	1x2 = 2	1x1 = 1
Keeping Track of Time Weight = 1	1x3 = 3	1x2 = 2	1x1 = 1
Getting Work Done on Time Weight = 1	1x3 = 3	1x2 = 2	1x1 = 1

Note: Analytic rubrics in subsequent chapters will weight some elements more heavily than others because some elements are more important than others.

Analytic Rubrics and Assessment Lists Compliment Each Other

First an analytic rubric is created that lists the traits of the behavior or work and describe the levels of quality for each trait. The analytic rubric can be displayed in the classroom all year and can be the center of discussions from time to time as students learn more about how they are expected to behave and perform.

The assessment list is a tool based on an analytic rubric, but is specifically focused on a particular activity or assignment. The assessment lists are also created to be an appropriate challenge to the particular students using it. Compare the analytic rubric in Figure 2.5 and the assessment list in Figure 2.8. The analytic rubric defines the general behaviors associated with managing time, and the assessment list is focused on managing time in a particular math graphing activity.

Using Assessment Lists

The act of creating the assessment list helps the teacher become more focused on what he expects of the students. The assessment list communicates and clarifies those expectations to the students.

Prior to the use of an assessment list, the teacher has verbally taught the students the behaviors or skills included on the assessment list. Although a student may not be good regarding a specific behavior or skill, the student understands what is meant by each item on the assessment list.

The students review the assessment list before they are about to engage in the behavior, skill, or work relevant to that assessment list. For example, the assessment list for managing time would be introduced at the beginning of a project that required good time-management skills. An assessment list for encouraging participation of a friend would be introduced before a cooperative learning activity.

As the students are engaged in the activity, the teacher uses the assessment list to refocus their attention on the specific behaviors and skills to which they should attend.

Immediately at the end of the activity, the teacher and the class review the assessment list and talk about the quality of their behavior or work. The teacher may ask, "How many points did you give yourself for using your assignment book and calendar for the math graphing project?," and, regardless of the response the students give, the teacher then says, "Show me your assignment book and calendar, and explain how you earned that many points." The teacher needs the students to judge their behavior or skill level and to justify that judgment with "evidence" of their actual performance.

Initially, when introducing the use of assessment lists, students may not be accurate in judging the quality of their own performance. A strategy is to focus on two or three items in which the students are very accurate. This kind of an assessment list item is called a "Sure Thing" because students will most likely do very well on it. When the students accurately assess their work on the "Sure Thing" items, a more difficult item can be introduced to the assessment list. Persistence and patience usually result in success. The key is to continue to ask students to show and/or explain the evidence that supports their self-assessment.

In the case of classroom behaviors presented in this chapter, students usually do not get individual assessment lists. Whole-group discussions are held using a large classroom assessment list poster or in a sentence-strip chart.

If a student is particularly weak in a behavior or skill, the student might receive an individualized two-item assessment list. One of the items would be on a behavior that the student has mastered, and the second item would focus on a behavior in need of improvement. This two-item assessment list is used in addition to the whole-class assessment list poster or sentence-strip chart.

Using Models of Desired Behaviors

"T" Charts, analytic rubrics, and assessment lists on their own are not sufficient to coach students to improve their performance. Students must see and hear examples, models, or benchmarks of excellent performance. Models can be in the format of a video; photographs; audio tape; or actual examples of student work such as drawings, writing, assignment books and calendars, constructions, and computer-generated products. Videos of students being respectful and courteous to classmates, a student's time plan that shows good time-management procedures, or a final draft of a persuasive letter can provide examples of expected levels of behavior. (If videos are not available, a substitute strategy is to use role-playing to demonstrate behaviors.)

Classroom discussions about what is seen and heard in these videos and/or samples of work help focus students' attention on what to do and how well to do it. Some teachers have their students use the assessment list to judge the quality of the behaviors presented in the videos and/or work samples so that the students experience connecting the items in the assessment list to actual performance.

Setting Goals (Standards of Performance) for Student Performance Regarding Desired Behaviors

The models or benchmarks of student performance show work above goal, at goal, and near goal. The actual levels of quality that define work above goal, at goal, and near goal are sometimes set by the school or school district, but they may be set by the classroom teacher in the absence of any other guidance.

Models or benchmarks of student behavior or work should set goals for performance. A video of a student doing an "above goal" job of encouraging a classmate to participate in a cooperative group learning activity, or a student's "at goal" drawing of a scene from a story with written explanation, help define what quality is.

Models of "at goal" and "near goal" levels of performance are sometimes used to help students compare and contrast between these levels and an "above goal" performance. Care must be taken not to offend students by showing their behavior or work as "near goal." Sometimes, simulations or skits are video-taped to be used as the "near goal" levels of performance. Sometimes, the teacher "creates" the flawed samples to use as a model of "near goal" so as not to embarrass any student.

Teachers save samples of student work from past years, with names removed, to use as models of excellent work and models with flaws.

Mantra of Self-Reflection: What?—So What?—Now What?

The goal of using assessment is to coach the student to take responsibility for accurately assessing their own work and then set and carry out goals to improve their performance. The teacher's job is to coach the students to learn to ask and answer these questions:

- **What** is my task?
- **What** is "at goal" work like? (Students who are already at goal should aspire to work that is above goal.)
- **So what** are the strengths of my work?
- **So what** do I need to improve?
- **Now what** am I going to do to get better?

Differentiating Instruction and Assessment

Students in our classrooms differ widely, and assessment lists and strategies to use them can be differentiated to meet some individualized needs. In some situations, the same assessment list can be used for the whole class. In other situations, two or three versions of the assessment list may be used. Regarding the general behavior of managing time, students may differ regarding their areas of deficiency. One assessment list may include the challenge item of "Did I use my assignment book and calendar to keep track of when my graphing project was due?" and another version of the assessment list may include the challenge item of "Did I print the words 'Graphing Project Due' on my calendar to show when the math graphing project was due?" The first version of this item is appropriate for students who are reasonably proficient at using assignment books and calendars. The second version is for students just beginning to use these time-management tools.

The assessment list enables the teacher to translate the analytic rubric into "developmentally appropriate" terms to help each student improve their performance.

The Long-Term Goal Regarding Using Assessment Lists

The ultimate goal of using assessment lists is for goes beyond helping students get good at using the assessment lists we create. The goal is for students to internalize the process of thinking about quality before they begin their work, during their work, and at the conclusion of their work. We want students to use the "assessment lists in their heads." Steps along the way to this goal include getting good at using assessment lists provided by teachers, helping to make assessment lists, making assessment lists, and using an internalized assessment list.

In the elementary grades we begin this process that empowers students to become motivated, independent learners who take responsibility for the quality of their behavior and work.

Glossary of Terms

Analytic Rubric: A type of assessment tool that lists all the specific attributes of a performance and provides narrative descriptions of several levels of performance for each of those attributes. An analytic rubric for a complex behavior such as "Persuasive Writing" may have six or more items. Four levels of quality are defined for each of those items.

An analytic rubric is created and used for one or more grade levels as a consistent framework to view student performance.

Assessment List: A type of assessment tool that lists a few of the many possible attributes of the performance. An assessment list for "Managing Time" may have only three or four items because that is the maximum number of items the students are ready to pay attention to at the time the assessment list is created. Assessment lists are written by the teacher, often with input from the students. Assessment lists are developed for specific tasks and are changed often as students master some behaviors or skills and shift their attention to new learning.

Although the analytic rubric, once created, remains unchanged for a long time, the assessment lists change often based on the behaviors and skills to which the students should attend.

Model: A model is an example of the behavior (active listening) or work (creating a story board and then writing the story) being examined with the help of an assessment tool. (Synonyms for the term "model" include example, benchmark, and standard of quality.) Models usually show the goal for the exhibition of the behavior or skill. Models for "flawed" work are sometimes used to help point out the strengths of the good work through comparing and contrasting models of excellence with the flawed examples.

Performance-Based Learning and Assessment: *Assessment* is the gathering of information about what students know and are able to do. Performance assessment focuses on the application of knowledge and skills. The strategies in this book are called "performance-based learning and assessment" because the activities used as the basis for assessment are both learning activities and opportunities to assess student performance.

Self-Assessment: Students use assessment lists and their knowledge of models (benchmarks) to identify their own strengths and needs. Teachers coach students to learn to be accurate self-assessors.

Self-Regulation: Through self-regulation, students set and carry-out goals to improve their performance. Teachers coach students to set realistic goals and action plans to improve. This drives the instruction for another cycle of work that culminates with another round of self-assessment and self-regulation.

Standards of Performance: Each type of behavior, such as managing time, encouraging friends to participate in group work, and writing, is manifested in a range of actual student performance. A standard of performance, i.e., standard of quality, is set to define the high goal towards which to strive. Models of student performance including videos of actual performance are used to define these standards of performance.

"T" Chart: A "T" Chart is a tool used by teachers to help students identify the specific outcomes of their behavior or work, which then can be used to create assessment tools.

3

A Framework for Reading Comprehension

Topics in This Chapter

- The reading comprehension framework from the National Assessment of Educational Progress (NAEP).
- Using the reading comprehension framework to create comprehension questions for fiction and nonfiction reading.

Levels of Reading Comprehension

Comprehension can be thought of as a continuum, from barely understanding the simple facts of a story to a deeper understanding of the author's "message" and how the story connects to the reader's own life. Likewise, for nonfiction, comprehension spans the range of understanding a few simple facts to a deeper understanding of concepts and their connection to other topics and life experiences.

This book uses a four-level framework for reading comprehension as described by the National Assessment of Educational Progress (NAEP). The first level is called **Initial Understanding** and refers to the degree to which students "literally" understand the basic facts of a book. At this level the students identify the main characters, describe the setting as shown in the illustrations, and retell the story. For nonfiction, Initial Understanding includes listing and describing facts from the text.

The second level of comprehension is called **Developing an Interpretation**. It refers to the degree to which students can use thinking skills such as predicting what comes next in the story, and finding evidence to show that a character exhibited an attribute such as friendship or bravery. For nonfiction, Developing an Interpretation includes explaining the meaning of the text and making predictions and generalizations from it.

The third level of comprehension is called **Making Connections**. It refers to the degree to which the students can use thinking skills, such as comparing one story to another, or comparing an event in a story to an event in their own lives. The connections are "text-to-me," "text-to-text," and "text-to-world." For nonfiction, Making Connections includes comparing and contrasting two or more people, places, or things based on information from two or more sources.

The fourth level of comprehension is called **Critical Stance**. For fiction books, one use of Critical Stance refers to the degree to which students form an opinion and support it. Here, the student judges or evaluates the author's or illustrator's work. This is where a student may share whether he liked or disliked the story, the characters, or the illustrations and be able to explain why. Another use of Critical Stance for fiction is for the student to evaluate or judge the soundness of the author's ideas and messages. Still another use of Critical Stance for fiction is for the student to extend the author's work through such activities as writing a new chapter or writing a new story with the same main character as in the original. To be successful in these "extensions," the student must have developed a critical understanding of the author's style.

For nonfiction books, one use of Critical Stance is to make and support judgments on the quality of the information, i.e., is it accurate, up-to-date, written by a creditable author, and objective? Another use of Critical Stance for nonfiction is to make and support judgments, evaluations, or ratings of: the plausibility of an idea or plan; clarity of an editorial or news article; soundness of a solution to a mathematical problem; or impact of a painting or musical performance.

Figure 3.1 shows the relationship among the four levels of comprehension. Initial Understanding is the foundation of comprehension because if you do not know the facts, the higher levels of comprehension will be more difficult to achieve. The other three levels extend beyond Initial Understanding. Developing an Interpretation, Making Connections, and Critical Stance represent higher-order thinking than Initial Understanding. Initial Understanding is the foundation on which higher-order thinking is based. Initial Understanding asks what you know and the other three levels of comprehension ask how you can use what you know.

Figure 3.1. Four Levels of Reading Comprehension

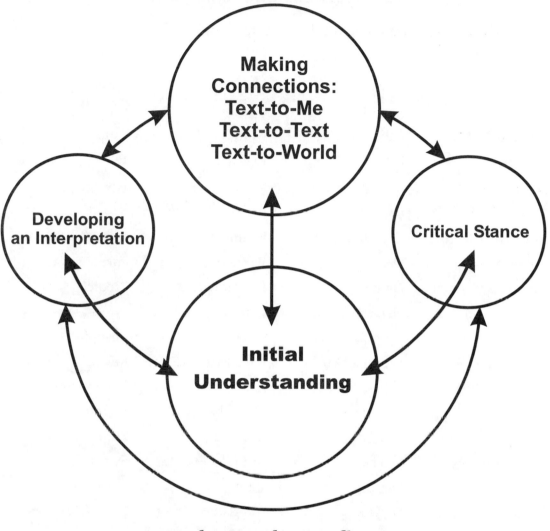

Verbs Used to Define
the Four Levels of Comprehension

Figure 3.2 presents a set of verbs for each of the four levels of comprehension. Note that Developing An Interpretation and Making Connections share the same verbs. Development An Interpretation ask the student to think about information from one source and Making Connections ask the student to think about information from two or more sources.

These verbs are used to create comprehension questions for fiction or nonfiction texts.

Figure 3.2. Verbs Used for the Reading Comprehension Framework

Initial Understanding (i.e., literal understanding)

Choose	Display	Locate	Retell
Complete	Draw	Make	Sequence
Compute	Identify	Match	Show
Demonstrate	Label	Name	State
Describe	List	Recall	Tell

Developing an Interpretation (using one source of information) and **Making Connections** (using multiple sources of information)

Add To	Correlate	Examine	Make Analogies
Amend	Decide	Explain	Paraphrase
Analyze	Deduce	Extrapolate	Predict
Apply	Defend	Forecast	Prioritize
Categorize	Describe:	Generalize	Respond
Challenge	• Cause/Effect	Give Evidence For	Revise
Classify	• Patterns	Guess	Summarize
Cluster	• Relationships	Hypothesize	Supplement
Combine	Design	Illustrate	Support
Compare	Devise	Induce	Synthesize
Complete	Discuss	Infer	Uncover
Conclude	Dissect	Integrate	Use Metaphors
Confirm	Document	Interpret	Use Similes
Construct	Draw Conclusions	Justify	
Contrast	Estimate	Make a Plan	

Critical Stance

Assess	Evaluate	Judge	Rate
Defend	Extend	Rank	Rule On
Dispute	Identify Error		

Selecting Verbs for Your Classroom

Figure 3.2 presents a long list of verbs. Teachers can choose a smaller collection of verbs on which to focus in their classroom. The collection must include verbs for all four levels of comprehension. For example, one fourth-grade teacher selected the following collection:

Initial Understanding

> describe, identify, list, locate, retell, sequence

Developing an Interpretation and Making Connections

> categorize, compare, contrast, describe cause/effect, describe patterns, estimate, explain, generalize, hypothesize, illustrate, infer, interpret, make analogies, paraphrase, predict, summarize

Critical Stance

> assess, defend, evaluate, extend, judge, rank

Developing an Interpretation uses the verbs with one information source, and Making Connections uses the same verbs with two or more information sources.

This collection was posted in the classroom and used in many contexts every day. These verbs are used for the development of comprehension questions and performance tasks, and they are also used more informally to engage students in all levels of comprehension during read-alouds and classroom discussions.

Creating Comprehension Questions for Fiction

Figure 3.3 is a menu of questions relating the four levels of thinking to the elements of a story. The menu was created by using some verbs in each of the four categories to make lists of ideas for questions. Those ideas were then transformed into questions. Figure 3.4 (page 42) shows a sample of a worksheet to create ideas and transform them into questions.

When teachers can share the menu in Figure 3.3 with their students, the students can create questions at all four levels of comprehension for use in their discussions of literature. Teachers show students how to use this menu to create a set of questions for a book. Becoming aware of the whole framework in this way helps the students develop a comprehensive view of comprehending a book.

Figure 3.5 (page 43) presents comprehension questions organized around the four levels of comprehension for several books of fiction. Figure 3.6 presents comprehension questions organized around the elements of a story. Although many questions could be created for each level of comprehension for each book, only one question at each level of comprehension is presented here for each book.

Figure 3.3. Menu of Questions Relating the Four Levels of Thinking to the Elements of a Story

Add the following to the questions as necessary: "Explain," "Find three details from the text to support your ideas." Add or exchange the word "illustrator" to selected questions that use the word "author."

LEVEL OF THINKING	CHARACTER *Who*	SETTING *Where, When*	EVENTS *What, How*	PURPOSE *Why*
Initial Understanding (i.e., describe, sequence, list)	1. Who is the main character? 2. Who are the other characters? 3. What words does the author use to describe _____ (name the character)?	1. Where does the story take place? 2. When does the story take place? 3. What words does the author use to describe the setting?	1. What are the main events in the story? 2. What happened in the beginning? in the middle? at the end? 3. What was the problem? (The problem may be obvious or it may need to be inferred.)	1. What does the title tell us about this story? 2. What does the cover illustration tell us about the story?
Developing An Interpretation (i.e., infer, predict, generalize, analyze cause and effect, compare, contrast)	1. How do you know that _____ (name the character) is _____ (state character trait such as friendly, brave, honest)? 2. If we know that _____ (name the character) is _____ (state the character trait) what do you think that _____ (name the character) would do if _____ (describe the new situation)? 3. How do you think that _____ (name a character) felt about _____ (name a character or an event)? 4. When _____ (name a character) said _____, what do you think he/she meant? 5. What do you think that _____ (name a character) was thinking when _____ (name an event)? 6. What do you think the word (or phrase) _____ means? How do you know?	1. What do you think the word (or phrase) _____ means? How do you know? 2. What is the most important thing about the setting? 3. Why was _____ (mention a part of the setting) a part of the setting? 4. How would the story have changed if _____ (mention a part of the setting) was left out of the story?	1. Why did _____ (describe the event) happen? 2. Why did _____ (name character) _____ (state event)? 3. What caused _____? 4. How did _____ (name a character) get _____ (name a thing)? 5. Why do you think that it was important that _____ happened in the story? 6. What do you think the word (or phrase) _____ means? How do you know? 7. At the end of the story, when _____ (describe an event or something said), what did it mean? 8. If _____ (name an event) had not happened, how would the story have turned out differently?	1. What lesson did the author want us to learn from this story? (This is the implicit purpose.) 2. What do you think the word (or phrase) _____ means? How do you know? 3. Why did the author tell us about _____ (describe what the author told) in this story? 4. How did the title of the story relate to the purpose of this story?

LEVEL OF THINKING	CHARACTER	SETTING	EVENTS	PURPOSE AND OVERALL
Making Connections (i.e., compare, contrast)	1. How was _____ (name a character) like (different from) _____ (name another character in the story)? 2. What was the relationship between _____ (name a character) and _____ (name another character)? 3. How is _____ (name the character) like _____ (name a character from another book)? 4. How is _____ (name the character) like you?	1. How is the setting for this story like the setting of _____ (name the other story)? 2. How is the setting for this story like _____ (name the real setting that the child experiences)?	1. How is the problem in this story like a problem in a story you have read before? 2. How is the problem in this story like a problem you may have had? 3. How is your experience like or different from a character's in this story? 4. What do you think would happen between _____ (name one character) and _____ (name another character) if _____ (describe a new situation that would require the two characters to solve a similar problem.) 5. If you were in this situation, what would you have done? Why?	1. How is the lesson of this story like the lesson from another story you have read? 2. How is the lesson of this story like a lesson you have learned in real life?
Critical Stance (i.e., judge, evaluate, rate)	1. Did the author do a good job of showing us that _____ (name the character) was _____ (state the character trait)? 2. Did the author do a good job of making _____ (name the character) seem like a real little boy / girl? 3. Did the author do a good job making _____ (name the character) an interesting character? 4. Did the author do a good job making _____ (name the character) believable? 5. Why did the author use details about _____ (name some aspect of the character)?	1. Did the author do a good job of making the setting seem real? 2. How did the author use _____ (state the literary device) to help you understand the setting? 3. Why did the author use details about _____ (name some aspect of the setting)? 4. Did the author do a good job making the setting believable?	1. Did the author do a good job of making the story interesting? 2. Did the author do a good job of presenting a problem and then showing how it was solved? 3. Did the author do a good job of telling about a problem that we could have? 4. If this story continued, what do you think would happen next? 5. How did the author use _____ (state the literary device) to make the story interesting to you? 6. Why did the author use details about _____ (name some aspect of the plot)? 7. Was this story as good as _____ (list the title of another story)? Explain.	1. Is the lesson of this story an important lesson to learn? 2. What do you think is important to the author? 3. What do you think the author is like as a person? 4. What customs and celebrations, are important to the author? 5. Was the title a good one for this story? 6. What would a better title be for this story? 7. Did the author do a good job making the story believable? 8. Did the author make any mistakes in telling this story? 9. How would you make this story better? 10. Overall, was this a good book? 11. Would you recommend this book to a friend? 12. Would you want to read other books by this author?

Figure 3.4. Creating Questions for Reading Comprehension

Level of Comprehension and Some Verbs for That Level	Ideas for Questions Related to the Characters of a Book	Comprehension Questions
Initial Understanding		
Describe, List, Sequence	• List the characters. • Describe the main character.	• Who is the main character? • Which words does the author use to describe the main character?
Developing an Interpretation		
Infer, Predict	• Infer the character traits of a character. • Infer how one character thinks or feels about another character. • Infer the motives or thoughts of a character. • Predict what a character would do in another situation.	• How do know that (main character) is brave? • How do you think that (main character) felt about (another character)? • What do you think that (main character) meant when he said _____? • What do you think that (main character) was thinking when he _____? • What would (main character) do if _____?
Making Connections		
Compare, Contrast	• Compare a character in one book to a character in another book. • Contrast a character to yourself.	• How is (main character in this story) the same as (main character from another story?) • How are you and (main character) the same or different?
Critical Stance		
Judge, Evaluate, Rate	• Judge the author's skill in creating a believable main character. • Evaluate the author's use of word choice to describe the main character. • Judge what the main character would do in another situation. • Rate how interesting the main character was.	• Did the author do a good job portraying (main character) as an eight-year-old? • Did the author do a good job of using descriptive language to paint a picture of (main character?) • What would (main character) do if he came to your school and was a student in your classroom? • How interesting was (main character?)

Figure 3.5. Sample Comprehension Questions Organized around the Four Levels of Comprehension

Add the following to the questions as necessary: *"Explain," "Find three details from the text to support your ideas."*				
	Level of Comprehension			
Book Title	*Initial Understanding*	*Developing an Interpretation*	*Making Connections*	*Critical Stance*
Coming Home	Who were the people in Langston Hughes' family and what did each one do? (list, describe)	How do you think Langston Hughes felt about writing? (infer)	What did Langston Hughes enjoy about Kansas City? What do you enjoy about your city? (compare)	Is the title, *Coming Home*, a good title for this story? Explain. (judge)
Sarah, Plain and Tall	Who was Sarah? (describe)	Was Sarah courageous and was she a kind person? (infer)	How is your house different from the house in which Sarah lived on the prairie? (contrast)	Did the author, Patricia MacLachlan, do a good job of describing life on the prairie? (evaluate)
Stone Fox	What was the problem that Grandfather had? (describe)	Summarize the difficult things that Willy did. (summarize)	How is the character Willy like a character in another book you have read? (compare)	Did the author, John Reynolds Gardiner, do a good job of making Willy seem like a real boy? (assess)
The Story of Ruby Bridges	What happened to Ruby when she wanted to go to school? (sequence)	Why did some people give Ruby such a hard time about going to school? (generalize)	What would happen if Ruby came to your school? (predict)	Did the author, Robert Coles, do a good job of showing that Ruby was a brave girl? (evaluate)

Figure 3.6. Sample Comprehension Questions Organized around the Elements of a Story

Add the following to the questions as necessary:
"Explain," "Find three details from the text to support your ideas."

IU = Initial Understanding   **DI** = Developing An Understanding
MC = Making Connections   **CS** = Critical Stance

Book Title	Elements of a Story			
	Setting	**Character**	**Events**	**Purpose**
Soup	Does the author do a good job of making the setting believable to you? (CS: evaluate)	How do you know that Souperman is a brave person? (DI: infer)	What happens in the beginning, middle, and ending of the story? (IU: sequence)	What was the author trying to teach us in this story? (DI: hypothesize)
Amber Brown Is Not a Crayon	What was the most important thing about the setting? (DI: explain)	What was the relationship between Amber and Justin? (DI: infer)	What would be another good title for this story? (DI: defend)	Is the lesson of this story an important lesson for us to learn? (MC: draw conclusion)
A Grain of Rice	What did the country look like where Pong Lo lived? (IU: describe)	Did the author do a good job showing that Pong Lo was a hard worker? (CS: evaluate)	Did the author do a good job of presenting the problem and then showing how Pong Lo tries to solve the problem? (CS: assess)	How is the lesson of this story like the lesson from another story you have read? (MC: compare)
I Have a Dream	How would the story be different if the story took place in a northern city? (DI: contrast, predict)	What would you do if your best friend's mother said you could not play with him or her? (MC: compare)	What is the most important event in the beginning of the story? (DI: explain)	How did the author tell us about prejudice? (MC: summarize)

Creating Comprehension Questions for Nonfiction

Comprehension questions for each of the four levels of comprehension are created for each nonfiction text in courses such as science and social studies. Figures 3.7 through 3.12 present examples of statements and questions. Note that a verb relevant to a specific level of comprehension is used to begin each statement. Each statement is transformed into a question. Teachers can use either the statement or the question as the basis of discussions and performance tasks.

Creating sets of statements and questions for nonfiction helps to ensure that the comprehension activities will address all four levels of comprehension. Notice in Figure 3.12, the Initial Understanding questions cover the Who, What, When, Where and How questions, and the Developing an Interpretation question covers the Why question. The Making Connection questions "connects" the reading about a heroine of the American Revolution to a previous lesson about Paul Revere, and the Critical Stance question focuses on the author's skills as a storyteller.

Figure 3.7. Statements and Questions: Beavers

Initial Understanding	
Describe how the beaver keeps its fur dry.	How does the beaver keep its fur dry?
Developing an Understanding	
Examine how the shape of the beaver's teeth help it do it's work.	How does the shape of the beaver's teeth help it do its work?
Making Connections	
Compare the beaver to other animals.	What other animals are similar to the beaver?
Critical Stance	
Judge the quality of the pictures and drawings in this book.	Do the pictures and drawings give you good information about beavers?

Figure 3.8. Dragonflies

Initial Understanding	
List the sequence of stages in the life cycle of a dragonfly.	What are the stages of the life cycle of a dragonfly?
Developing an Understanding	
Contrast a dragonfly and a damselfly.	What are the differences between a dragonfly and a damselfly?
Making Connections	
Generalize the similarities among ants, butterflies, beetles, and dragonflies.	How are the insects we have studied (ants, butterflies, beetles and dragonflies) all the same?
Critical Stance	
Evaluate the information about how a dragonfly catches and eats its food.	Did the author do a good job using text, pictures, and drawings of showing how a dragonfly catches and eats its food?

Figure 3.9. Muskrats

Initial Understanding	
Draw a picture of the type of place where a muskrat lives.	What does the land look like where muskrats live?
Developing an Understanding	
Predict what would happen to muskrats during a long, severe drought.	What would happen to muskrats if there was a very long, severe drought?
Making Connections	
Explain how beavers and muskrats build their homes to protect themselves from other animals.	How do beavers and muskrats build their homes so that they are protected from other animals?
Critical Stance	
Defend the name "muskrat" for this animal?	Why is the name "muskrat" a good name for this animal?

Figure 3.10. Worms

Initial Understanding	
Compute how many average earthworms it would take to equal in length one giant Australian earthworm.	How many average earthworms would it take to equal the length of one giant Australian earthworm?
Developing an Understanding	
Justify the name "soil making machine" to describe an earthworm.	Why is the name "soil making machine" a good name for an earthworm?
Making Connections	
Give evidence for earthworms living somewhere in your school's property.	How do you know that earthworms are living in your school's property?
Critical Stance	
Defend or dispute this statement, "The author did not give very much information about the external and internal parts of an earthworm."	Did the author do a good job of teaching you about the internal and external parts of an earthworm?

Figure 3.11. Heroines of the American Revolution— Mary Linder Murray: The Woman Who Stopped the British Army

Initial Understanding	
Locate on a map where Mary Linder Murray lived.	Where did Mary Linder Murray live?
Developing an Understanding	
Infer the importance of Mary's hospitality to the British.	Why was Mary's hospitality to the British important to the Patriot army?
Making Connections	
Hypothesize what would have happened to the American Revolution if there were no brave women Patriots.	How important were the women Patriots to the American Revolution?
Critical Stance	
Judge how well the story showed that Mary Linder Murray was smart and brave.	How well did the author show that Mary Linder Murray was smart and brave?

Figure 3.12. Heroines of the American Revolution— Sybil Ludington, the Female Paul Revere

Initial Understanding	
Describe what Sybil Ludington did.	Who was Sybil Ludington? Where did she live? What did she do? When did she do it? How did she do it?
Developing an Interpretation	
Give evidence for how important Sybil Ludington's ride was.	Why was Sybil Ludington's ride so important? What is the evidence?
Making Connections	
Compare and **contrast** the ride of Paul Revere and the ride of Sybil Ludington.	How were the rides of Paul Revere and Sybil Ludington the same and different?
Critical Stance	
Evaluate how the author made the story of Sybil Ludington exciting.	What writing strategies did the author use to make her story of Sybil Ludington exciting?

All Students Should Encounter All Four Levels of Comprehension

Teachers discover that when they create questions without being aware of the four levels of comprehension, their questions focus mostly on Initial Understanding. They might include some Developing an Interpretation and/or Making Connections questions, but often do not address Critical Stance at all.

A systematic use of the four levels of comprehension for fiction and nonfiction will ensure that teaching and learning is a balance of these levels of comprehension.

A practice to be avoided is to give the lower-performing students Initial Understanding questions and give the higher-performing students questions in the other "higher order thinking" levels. All students should encounter all four levels of comprehension in each unit of study.

Students Can Help Create Questions for Their Reading

Teachers can instruct students in how to use the comprehension verbs to create questions. After the class has finished reading, the teacher models how to create at least one question in each of the four levels of comprehension. Then the students, working in cooperative groups, create one more question for each of those four levels of comprehension. This strategy helps the students become aware of the whole reading comprehension framework, and they are more likely to consciously think about the facts (Initial Understanding), what they mean (Developing an Interpretation), how they are connected to other lessons (Making Connections), and how well the author is doing his job (Critical Stance.)

Comprehension Questions Are the Beginning Point to Create Performance Tasks

Figures 3.3 through 3.12 present questions for fiction and nonfiction. These questions are "ideas" for performance tasks. The transformation of a question into a fully developed performance task with an assessment rubric or list is explained in subsequent chapters.

References

Coles, R. (1995). *The Story of Ruby Bridges* (G. Ford, Illus.). New York: Scholastic.

Cooper, F. (1994). *Coming home: From the life of Langston Hughes*. New York: The Putnam & Grosset Group.

Dingwall, L. (1986). *Muskrats*. Danbury, CT: Grolier.

Gardiner, J. R. (1980). *Stone Fox*. New York: HarperCollins.

Green, J. (1999). *Dragonflies*. Danbury, CT: Grolier.

Green, J. (1999). *Worms*. Danbury, CT: Grolier.

Kelsey, E. (1986). *Beavers*. Danbury, CT: Grolier.

McLachan, P. (1984). *Sarah, Plain and Tall*. New York: HarperCollins.

Silcox-Jarrett, D. (1998). *Heroines of the American Revolution*. Chapel Hill, NC: Green Angel Press.

4

Teaching and Assessing Reading Comprehension of Fiction Through Drawing

Topics in This Chapter

♦ Strategies for using a framework for reading comprehension that focuses on thinking-skill verbs to make performance tasks that ask students to draw and present orally.

♦ Strategies to make analytic rubrics and assessment lists for judging the quality of drawings and oral presentations.

♦ Strategies to use performance tasks and assessment tools in the context of language arts lessons.

Note: A glossary of terms is at the end of the chapter.

Careful Observation Is a Foundation for Understanding

Careful reading for literal understanding and careful observation of illustrations are the foundation for deeper levels of understanding. Inferences, comparisons, and evaluations can only be done if the basic information in the text is understood. In this chapter, performance tasks at all four levels of comprehension ask the student to make drawings to show their understanding of the information in the books. Then students are asked to describe their drawings to their classmates. Assessment lists are used for both the drawings and the oral presentations.

Drawing and Oral Presentations of the Drawings Are a Form of Pre-Writing

Pre-writing is an opportunity to collect, organize and process information to be used in the writing. Drawings, and oral presentations of the drawings, are used as the final products of the performance tasks in this chapter and as preliminary steps—pre-writing—in subsequent chapters.

Principles and Elements of Design for Drawings

An artist has a concept in mind for his drawing. The concept might be to convey something like "the beauty of a tree," "a scary feeling," "a proud moment," or the "love of a family member." Figure 4.1 presents a chart of the principles and elements of design. The student artist makes decisions about how to use a principle, such as "Emphasis," to help present the concept. For example, the student artist may wish to emphasize a brave action taken by a character. Then the artist uses an element such as color to carry out the principle. For example, strong, bold, bright colors may help provide the emphasis to the brave action that is to be highlighted.

The chart in Figure 4.1 can be a source of ideas for assessment list elements. It is presented in a matrix form so that decisions can be made as to which elements will be used to accomplish a given principle. For example, a teacher has used the chart in Figure 4.1 to select the principle of "Emphasis" and the elements of "color" and "value" to accomplish that principle. The performance task and its assessment list will incorporate the use of color and value to accomplish emphasis. Figure 4.7 presents a performance task entitled, *What the Children Did to Keep from Being Bored*. Figure 4.8 presents the assessment list for that task, and element "2" asks, "Did I use strong, bright colors to emphasize what the children did to keep from being bored?" The information in the assessment list is consistent with, but more specific than, the information in the analytic rubric for drawings.

Collaborate with an art teacher when you use principles and elements of design as part of the instruction and assessment of student drawing.

Principles of Design

- ♦ **Pattern**: A pattern refers to the combination of lines, colors, and shapes used to show real or imaginary things. This is also achieved by repeating a line, color, or shape, etc.
- ♦ **Movement**: Movement refers to the arrangement of objects in a drawing that creates an impression of slow or fast movement
- ♦ **Balance**: Balance refers to the equalization of elements. Types of balance include symmetrical (equal on both sides), asymmetrical (bal-

anced but unequal in number), and radial or central balance (spokes on a wheel or rays on a sun.)

- **Unity**: Unity refers to the sense of oneness or wholeness in a work of art.
- **Contrast**: Contrast refers to different values, colors, textures, and other elements in a work of art used to achieve emphasis and interest.
- **Rhythm**: Rhythm indicates the type of movement in an artwork or design that is often represented by repeating shapes.
- **Emphasis**: Emphasis defines a central focal point or points to which the eyes are drawn.

Elements of Design Are Used to Accomplish the Principles

- **Texture**: Texture refers to the surface quality of an artwork—the way it "feels," such as rough, smooth, bumpy, fuzzy, hard, or soft.
- **Shape**: Shape is defined by a two-dimensional and enclosed space. All geometric shapes are included. Organic shapes are freeform or shapes from nature, such as the maple leaf or pine tree shapes.
- **Form**: Form refers to a three-dimensional, enclosed volume, such as a cylinder, cube, or sphere.
- **Line**: Line may be two-dimensional, such as a pencil line on paper, or may be a three-dimensional line using a rope or wire.
- **Value**: Value refers to the lightness or darkness of a color.
- **Space**: Space refers to either the positive area of an object or the negative space where the object isn't.
- **Color**: Color refers to the hue (red, yellow, violet). The primary colors are blue, yellow, and red. The secondary colors are green, orange, and violet.

Figure 4.1. Principles and Elements of Design Used to Help the Artist Convey His Concepts and Ideas to an Audience

Principles of Design	Elements of Design Used to Accomplish Principles						
	Texture	Shape	Form	Line	Color	Value	Space
Pattern							
Movement							
Balance							
Unity							
Contrast							
Rhythm							
Emphasis					X	X	

Analytic Rubrics for Drawing and Oral Presentation

Figures 4.2 and 4.3 (pages 55, 56) present analytic rubrics that help teachers consider three levels of performance for the elements of drawing and speaking. Chapter 2 described a strategy to weight some elements in an analytic rubric. All of the elements in the analytic rubrics in Figures 4.2 and 4.3 have the same weight, i.e., all elements are of equal weight, but a teacher could assign different weights to some elements to emphasize the importance of one or more of the elements in those rubrics.

Figure 4.9 (page 69) shows how the elements in the rubric in Figure 4.2 could be weighted to show that some elements are more important than other elements.

Framing Ideas for Performance Tasks Using the Thinking-Skill Verbs

A first step in creating performance tasks for a book is to create at least one idea for each of the four levels of reading comprehension. Figure 4.4 (page 57) presents a menu of ideas for performance tasks for several books.

Figure 4.2. Analytic Rubric for Drawings

Items	Levels of Performance		
	Terrific Weight = 3	Okay Weight = 2	Needs Work Weight = 1
On the Topic Weight = 1	The drawing is clearly on the topic of the assignment.	Most of the drawing is on the topic of the assignment.	The drawing is off the topic.
Shows Details Weight = 1	Just the right amount of details are used to communicate the information.	Either too many or too few details are used.	There are no details, or there are so many details that they obscure the main point of the drawing.
Uses Colors Weight = 1	The student uses colors expertly for emphasis, contrast, or another purpose.	The student uses colors for emphasis, contrast, or another purpose.	The student does not use colors well according to the purpose of the assignment.
Uses Shapes and Forms Weight = 1	The student uses shapes and forms correctly.	Most of the shapes and forms are correct.	Many of the shapes and forms are not correct.
Uses Proportion Weight = 1	The proportions are correct.	The proportions are mostly correct.	The proportions are mostly incorrect.
Shows Pattern, Movement, Balance, Unity, Contrast, Rhythm, and Emphasis Weight = 1	The student is very accomplished at using these principles to accomplish the purpose of the task.	The student is proficient at using these principles to accomplish the purpose of the task.	The student does not use these principles to accomplish the purpose of the task.
Shows Foreground/ Middleground/ Background Weight = 1	The drawing clearly uses foreground, middleground, and background.	The student uses two of these levels, such as foreground and background only.	The student only uses one level—no three-dimensional effect at all.
Uses Labels and Words Weight = 1	Labels are descriptive and correct if needed.	Labels are mostly descriptive and correct.	Labels are lacking or are not descriptive and/or are incorrect.
Uses the Paper Weight = 1	Uses the entire paper well.	Uses most of the paper well.	Does not use the paper well.
Overall Impact and Creativity Weight = 1	Wow!!! It really gets my attention.	It gets my attention.	It is not attention-grabbing.
Is Neat Weight = 1	Very neat.	Neat.	Not neat.

Figure 4.3. Analytic Rubric for Oral Descriptions of Drawings

Items	Levels of Performance		
	Terrific Weight = 3	Okay Weight = 2	Needs Work Weight = 1
On the Topic Weight = 1	The presentation is entirely on the topic of the drawing. The student very clearly answers the question about the drawing.	Most of the presentation is about the drawing. The student answers the question about the drawing.	The student strays off-topic.
Presents the Drawing Weight = 1	The student shows the drawing for all to see clearly.	The drawing is shown so that most of the students can see it.	The drawing is not presented well—not many students can see it.
Describes/ Explains the Details of the Drawing Weight = 1	The student includes many details in the description of the drawing.	The student includes some details in the description.	The student uses few or no details.
Organization Weight = 1	The oral presentation is very well organized.	The oral presentation is organized.	The oral presentation is not organized.
Higher-Order Thinking (as defined by the comprehension level verb) Weight = 1	The student's description does a very good job of showing the thinking required in the task.	The student's description does a good job of showing the thinking required in the task.	The student's description does not show the thinking required in the task.
Uses Descriptive Language Weight = 1	The student uses many descriptive words to describe the drawing.	The student uses some descriptive language.	The student uses little or no descriptive language.
Uses a Loud, Group-Sharing Voice Weight = 1	The student uses a loud, group-sharing voice throughout the presentation so all can hear.	The student uses a loud, group-sharing voice most of the time and can be heard by most.	The student's voice is too quiet and cannot be heard.

Figure 4.4. Menu of Ideas for Performance Tasks

Book Title	Levels Of Comprehension			
	Initial Understanding	Developing an Interpretation	Making Connections	Critical Stance
More Stories Julian Tells (A Day When Frogs Wear Shoes)	Draw a picture that shows what kind of a day it is when frogs wear shoes. (describe)	Draw a picture that shows what the children did to not be bored. (infer)	Draw a picture of what you do to not be bored. (compare)	Did the author do a good job describing what frogs really look like? Draw a picture that shows what the author said frogs look like. (assess)
Fantastic Mr. Fox	Draw and label a picture of what the farmers eat. (list)	Draw a picture of Mr. Fox's house. (infer, illustrate)	Draw a picture that compares the farmers to the wolf in the *Three Little Pigs.* (compare)	Did the author do a good job of showing that Mr. Fox was smart? Draw a picture to show what you think. (judge)
Every Living Thing (A Pet)	Draw a picture that shows what Emma's parents gave her as a pet. (describe)	Draw a picture that shows how Emma felt when Joshua was sick. (deduce)	Draw a picture of a time that you took care of an animal. Draw the picture so it shows what you did and how you felt. (illustrate)	Did the author use good descriptive language to describe what the fish looked like inside the aquarium? Draw a picture of the fish in the aquarium based on the author's description. (evaluate)
James and the Giant Peach	Draw a sequence of pictures to show the most important events in the story. (sequence)	Draw a picture that shows which characters are kind and which characters are unkind. (classify)	Draw a picture to show how James of *James and the Giant Peach* and Jack of *Jack in the Beanstalk* are the same and different. (compare and contrast)	Did the author do a good job of creating interesting characters? Draw a picture to show what you think. (evaluate)

| Book Title | Levels Of Comprehension | | | |
	Initial Understanding	Developing an Interpretation	Making Connections	Critical Stance
My Father's Dragon	Draw a picture of how Elmer got to the Wild Island. (sequence)	Draw a picture that shows how the baby dragon feels about his life on Wild Island. (infer, explain)	This dragon was friendly and brave. What other stories have you read about dragons? Pick a dragon from another story and draw a picture that compares it to this dragon. (compare)	Would this story make a great animated movie? Draw a picture that would be used to advertise this story if it were an animated movie. (assess)
Abel's Island	Draw a picture that shows two ideas Able had for getting off the island. (list)	Did Able have an easy time or a hard time living on the island? Draw a picture that shows what you think? (justify)	Able had his wife's scarf to help him feel better. What kinds of things do real children have to help them feel better? (generalize)	Should this author get an award for the use of descriptive language? Draw a picture based on some of the descriptive language. (judge)
Go Fish	Draw a picture of what Thomas and his grandfather took to go fishing. (list)	Draw a picture that shows one reason why Thomas loved his grandfather. (infer, decide)	Draw a picture that compares what Julian (*More Stories Julian Tells*) did and what Thomas (*Go Fish*) did to keep from being bored. (infer, compare)	Did the author tell enough interesting things about Thomas and his Grandfather to make the story interesting for you to read? Draw a picture of a part of the story that you thought was most interesting. (judge)

Creating Performance Tasks

Once ideas are generated for tasks, one or more of them can be turned into performance tasks with assessment lists. It is important that students be engaged in all four levels of reading comprehension: *Initial Understanding, Developing an Interpretation, Making Connections*, and *Critical Stance*. Teachers can frame many short discussion questions around the four levels of comprehension and create one or two performance tasks for a particular book. Over the course of using several books, performance tasks will address all four levels of comprehension.

Performance Tasks and Their Assessment Lists

Initial Understanding of *James and the Giant Peach*

Figure 4.5 (page 64) presents a performance task entitled, *Storyboard for James and the Giant Peach*. It is at the Initial Understanding level because it simply asks the students to draw the six most important events in the story.

Figure 4.6 (page 65) presents the assessment list for the performance task in Figure 4.5. Each item in the assessment list is worth three points. No one item has been given a weight greater than any other item. The assessment lists for other performance tasks in this chapter show that some items are given greater weights than other items.

Developing an Interpretation of *More Stories Julian Tells (A Day When Frogs Wear Shoes)*

Figure 4.7 (page 66) presents a performance task entitled, *What the Children Do to Keep from Being Bored*. This task is at the Developing an Interpretation level because it asks the students to make inferences from one information source—the story.

Figure 4.8 (page 67) presents the assessment list for the performance task in Figure 4.7. Some of the items in this assessment list are given greater weights than other items. Figure 4.9 (page 69) uses the framework of the analytic rubric for drawings to show how the items are weighted. Figure 4.10 (page 70) presents the assessment list for the oral presentation of this drawing.

Making Connections with *Abel's Island*

Figure 4.11 (page 71) presents the performance task entitled, *Dragons*, which is a Making Connections task because it asks the student to compare the dragon in Abel's Island to another dragon in a book, movie, or video.

Figure 4.12 (page 72) presents the assessment list for that task. Some items have been weighted heavily. For example, items 1, 2, 4, and 6 each have the weight of "12," whereas the other items have the weight of "6."

Critical Stance of *Fantastic Mr. Fox*

Figure 4.13 (page 73) presents the task entitled, *How Did the Author Show That Mr. Fox Was Smart?* This is a Critical Stance task because it asks the student to judge the skill of the author in creating a character that appears smart to the reader.

Figure 4.14 (page 74) presents the assessment list for this task. Some of the items have been given very heavy weights. For example, item 1 has the weight of "15" because the teacher wanted to emphasize the importance of drawing a picture that was clearly on the topic of how the author made Mr. Fox appear smart. Item 2 has the weight of "12" because the teacher wanted to emphasize the importance of showing details in the drawing.

Developing An Interpretation for *Go Fish*

Figure 4.15 (page 75) presents the performance task entitled, *A Loving Family*, which is a Developing an Interpretation task because it is asking the student to make and support an inference about what Grandfather did to show his love for Thomas.

In this task, there is no assessment list because the teacher plans to work with the class to create the assessment list that each student will then use. The students have had experience with the analytic rubric for drawing, and they have completed several performance tasks and assessment lists about drawing. Based on that experience, the students can suggest items for the new assessment list for the drawing that shows what Grandfather did to show his love for Thomas.

Making Assessment Lists for the Performance Tasks

The following are some guidelines for making assessment lists for specific performance tasks:

- ♦ **Use The Analytic Rubric:** Each assessment list is based on an analytic rubric. The assessment list highlights specific items from that rubric. The analytic rubric should be enlarged to poster size and displayed in the classroom so that students can remind themselves of what Terrific, Okay, and Needs Work means for each item in that analytic rubric.
- ♦ **The Purpose of Assessment Lists:** The purpose of an assessment list is to get the students to pay attention to as much as they will pay at-

tention to. The number of elements and the wording of each item must challenge the students without overwhelming them.

♦ **Number of Items in Assessment Lists:** In the beginning, an assessment list may consist of only two or three items because that is all the students will be able to pay attention to. The assessment list in Figure 4.6 has seven items on it. Students just beginning to use an assessment list may find that seven items are too many to pay close attention to. An appropriate assessment list for them might only contain four items. When the students are more experienced, the assessment list can expand to be more challenging.

♦ **Items Related to Task Content:** Each assessment list must have at least one item that is directly related to the content of the performance task. Item number one in the assessment list in Figure 4.8 asks, "Did I show one thing the three children did to keep from being bored?"

♦ **Items Related to Task Process Skills:** Assessment lists of more than one item would also include items relevant to the process skills important to the task. Items number two and five in the assessment list in Figure 4.14 ask about the degree to which the drawing is detailed and the degree to which the student has used foreground, middleground, and background. Item number seven in that same assessment list is about a work habit and asks, "Is my work neat?" All of these items are about processes important to the quality of the drawing.

♦ **Use the Analytic Rubric to Generate Items:** The analytic rubric in Figure 4.2 examines the levels of quality for the items of a drawing. Item number four in the assessment list shown in Figure 4.12 asks, "Did I use details in both of my drawings?" and is derived from the second specific behavior in the analytic rubric for drawing shown in Figure 4.2.

♦ **Use the Principles and Elements of Design to Generate Items:** Item two in the assessment list in Figure 4.8 asks, "Did I use strong, bright colors to emphasize what the children were doing to keep from being bored?," and is derived from the chart on Elements and Principles of Design in Figure 4.1. Collaboration between regular classroom teachers and art teachers in the use of the Principles and Elements of Design will support the improvement of student performance.

♦ **"Sure Thing" Items:** Some items must be about what the students will find easy to do because of their knowledge and skills. All the assessment lists for drawings in this chapter include a "sure thing" item that asks, "Did I use details in my drawing?" The teachers who created these assessment lists saw that their students were good at including details in their drawings. Because the class had spent time seeing and talking about examples of drawings that used just the right amount of details, the students were "Terrific" at using details.

♦ **"Challenge" Items:** One or two items in the assessment list should be a challenge for the students, i.e., something that students will find somewhat difficult to do. Item number four in the assessment list in Figure 4.14 asks, "Did I use proportion correctly?" The students will need considerable instruction about what this means before the task and assessment list are used. Unless students get prior instruction regarding challenge items, they will be unable to judge their own work in the way the challenge item calls for.

After more experience with the use of proportion, this skill will become a "sure thing" on subsequent assessment lists, and new "challenge" items will be added.

♦ **The Specificity of Items:** Challenge elements must be stated in very detailed and specific terms. The following sequence of assessment list elements, addressing the use of color to provide emphasis in a drawing, goes from a very specific statement to a general statement.

  • Did I use strong, bright colors to show how Mr. Fox was brave?
  • Did I use color to show how Mr. Fox was brave?
  • Did I use color for emphasis?

The first item in the sequence would be used for students just learning about how to use color to provide emphasis. The second item in the sequence would be used only after the students had a very good understanding that using color for emphasis means using strong, bold, bright colors. The third item in the list would be used only after students had a very good understanding that the use of color is important when creating emphasis in a drawing. Students may need to use the most specific version of this item many times before they are ready for a more general version.

♦ **Put Items in Question Format:** The act of self-assessment is like asking questions to yourself about your work. Therefore, the assessment list items are put into question format to model that "internal conversation inside your mind."

♦ **Simple Versus Complex Items:** A simple item in an assessment list might be, "Did I use details?" Whereas a more complex element involves two or more items such as, "Did I use details and geometric shapes in my drawing?" Simple items are best for young students.

♦ **Involve Students in Helping to Create Assessment Lists:** The point of assessment lists is to coach students to take responsibility for assessing their own work and improving their performance. When possible, the students should be involved in conversations to create assessment lists.

After the students are experienced in using several assessment lists, for example making drawings of some aspect of a story, the teacher might work with the whole group to create an assessment list for the drawing required in the next performance task.

Assessment Lists for Drawings and for Oral Descriptions of Drawings

Each task in this chapter includes an assessment list for a student's drawing. The first task, *Storyboard for James and the Giant Peach*, has an assessment list for the student's oral description of the drawing. Subsequent performance tasks do not include an assessment list for oral presentations. A large poster of the assessment list for oral presentations could be displayed in the room and used whenever there is an oral presentation.

How Students Use Assessment Lists

Before the student uses an assessment list, he or she has discussed the analytic rubric with the teacher and his classmates. Each item in that rubric is explained and modeled through student work samples that show Terrific and Okay work. Care is taken not to embarrass anyone through the display of his work. Work from previous years, with the name removed, can be used.

When the performance task is about to begin, the assessment list is distributed, and the teacher explains it to the students. Assessment lists are often introduced as whole-group activities by projecting a transparency of the list on a screen for all to see. When the teacher feels that the students are comfortable with how assessment lists work, the students receive their own assessment list to complete. The students refer to the assessment list as they work, and they do a final self-assessment when their work is completed. Then the teacher assesses the child's work on the same assessment list. The teacher also writes brief comments such as "I agree," "Look at the picture of _____ (the character)," or "I like the way you showed details."

The assessment list helps both the student and the teacher focus on specific components of the work. These assessment lists are then used during conferences with the student. Student work with completed assessment lists is useful information to share during parent-teacher conferences.

Figure 4.5. Performance Task:
Storyboard for *James and the Giant Peach*

Background

The story, *James and the Giant Peach*, is an exciting story from the beginning to the end. A playwright who lives near your school is thinking about making a school play based on this story. What do you think the most important parts of the story are?

Task

Your task is to draw six pictures that show the most important parts of the story.

Audience

You will show your pictures to a playwright who is thinking about making a play from the story.

Purpose

The purpose of your pictures is to show the playwright how the story could be a great play.

Procedure

1. Review the assessment list for this task.
2. Make some simple sketches to plan which parts of the story you will use for your six pictures.
3. Select the six parts of the story you will use for your pictures.
4. Make your six drawings.
5. Use the assessment list to assess your own work.
6. Turn in your work along with the assessment list showing your self-assessment.

Figure 4.6. Performance Task Assessment List: Storyboard for *James and the Giant Peach*

Item	Assessment Points Possible	Points Earned	
		Assessed by Self	Assessed by Teacher
1. Did I draw two pictures that showed two important events in the beginning of the story?	3	_____	_____
2. Did I draw two pictures that showed two important events in the middle of the story?	3	_____	_____
3. Did I draw two pictures that showed two important events in the ending of the story?	3	_____	_____
4. Did I show details in each of my six pictures?	3	_____	_____
5. Did I use foreground, middleground, and background in each picture?	3	_____	_____
6. Did I use strong, vivid colors to emphasize the action in each picture?	3	_____	_____
7. Is my work neat?	3	_____	_____
Total	**21**	_____	_____

Terrific = 3,   Okay = 2,   Needs Work = 1

Figure 4.7. Performance Task:
What the Children Do to Keep from Being Bored

Background

It was a hot day and Julian, Huey, and Gloria wondered what they would do to keep from being bored.

Task

Your task is to draw a picture of something the three children did to keep from being bored.

Audience

Your picture is for a collection of pictures we are making on the bulletin board for parents' night.

Purpose

Your picture will show parents what children like to do to keep from being bored.

Procedure

1. Review the assessment list to see what you need to pay attention to.
2. Find the parts of the story that tell you what the children did to keep from being bored.
3. Pick the thing you like best about how the children kept from being bored.
4. Draw a picture of what the children did to keep from being bored.
5. Use the assessment list to assess your own work.
6. Turn in your work along with the assessment list showing your self-assessment.

Figure 4.8. Performance Task Assessment List:
What the Children Do to Keep from Being Bored

		Points Earned	
Item	Assessment Points Possible	Assessed by Self	Assessed by Teacher
1. Did I show one thing the three children did to keep from being bored?	12	_____	_____
2. Did I use strong, bright colors to emphasize what the children were doing to keep from being bored?	3	_____	_____
3. Did I show details?	6	_____	_____
4. Did I use foreground, middleground, and background in the composition of my drawing?	3	_____	_____
5. Did I use the whole space of my paper?	3	_____	_____
6. Is my work neat?	3	_____	_____
Total	**30**	_____	_____

For item 1 in this assessment list, Terrific *work receives a score of 12;* Okay *work receives a score of 8, and* Needs Work *receives a score of no more than 4.*

This assessment list, Figure 4.8, shows that some elements have greater weights than other elements.

Figure 4.9 (page 69) shows how the weights for each element were determined.

How Points Were Assigned to the Items
in the Assessment List in Figure 4.8

The analytic rubric in Figure 4.2 was used as the basis for creating the assessment list in Figure 4.8. The rubric in Figure 4.2 shows that a rating of "Terrific" has a weight of 3, the rating of "Okay" has a rating of 2, and the rating of "Needs Work" has a rating of 1. Each of the elements down the left-hand column has a rating of 1. But other ratings could be given to individual ratings. The rubric for drawings in Figure 4.9 shows how different weights have been assigned to various elements.

The elements of being "On the Topic" and "Shows Details" are considered most important and are weighted accordingly. Four of the items, including "Uses Shapes and Forms" were not used in the specific assessment list shown in Figure 4.8. Not every item in a rubric is used in every assessment list because the assessment list might be too long. Each assessment list includes two or three items that are "Sure Things" to reinforce what the students do well, and each assessment list includes one or two "Challenges" to help improve performance.

Each time an assessment list is created and points are assigned to each of its items, the teacher decides which items from the rubric to use and what the weight of the chosen items should be.

Figure 4.9. Using a Rubric to Develop an Assessment List

Items	Levels of Performance		
	Terrific Weight = 3	Okay Weight = 2	Needs Work Weight = 1
On the Topic Weight = 4	4x3 = 12	8	4
Shows Details Weight = 2	2x3 = 6	4	2
Uses Colors Weight = 1	1x3 = 3	2	1
Shows Foreground/ Middleground/ Background Weight = 1	1x3 = 3	2	1
Uses the Paper Weight = 1	1x3 = 3	2	1
Is Neat Weight = 1	1x3 = 3	2	1
Total	**30**	**20**	**10**

Figure 4.10. Performance Task Assessment List:
Oral Presentation for the Drawing of
What the Children Do to Keep from Being Bored

	Item	Assessment Points Possible	Points Earned Assessed by Self	Assessed by Teacher
1.	Did I show my drawing so that everyone could see it as I talked?	3	_____	_____
2.	Did I stay on the topic of what the children did to keep from being bored?	3	_____	_____
3.	Did I describe the details I showed in my drawing?	9	_____	_____
4.	Did I use descriptive words?	6	_____	_____
5.	Did I use a loud, group-sharing voice?	6	_____	_____
	Total	27	_____	_____

Note: The assessment list for giving oral descriptions of the drawing to the class will not be repeated in this chapter. Other assessment lists for oral descriptions may focus on other elements, and may weight elements differently.

Figure 4.11. Performance Task: Dragons

Background

There was a dragon in the book, *My Father's Dragon*. You have read other books, and seen movies and videos, with stories about dragons. Are all dragons the same?

Task

Your task is to draw a picture of the dragon in *My Father's Dragon* and to draw a picture of a dragon from any other book, movie, or video.

Audience

Your pictures will be displayed in a bookstore or video rental store.

Purpose

The purpose of your pictures is get people interested in dragons.

Procedure

1. Review the assessment list for this task.
2. Draw a picture of the dragon from the story, *My Father's Dragon*.
3. Select a dragon from another book, movie, or video.
4. Draw a picture of that dragon.
5. Use the assessment list to assess your work.
6. Turn in your work along with the assessment list showing your self-assessment.

Figure 4.12. Performance Task Assessment List:
Dragons

Item	Assessment Points Possible	Points Earned	
		Assessed by Self	Assessed by Teacher
1. Did I draw a picture of the dragon from the story, *My Father's Dragon*?	12	_____	_____
2. Did I draw a picture of a dragon from another book, movie, or video?	12	_____	_____
3. Did I write the name of the book, movie, or video on each of my two drawings?	6	_____	_____
4. Did I use details in both of my drawings?	12	_____	_____
5. Did I use shapes and forms to emphasize the actions of the dragons?	6	_____	_____
6. Did I use strong, bold colors to emphasize the action of the dragons?	12	_____	_____
7. Is my work neat?	6	_____	_____
Total	**66**	_____	_____

Figure 4.13. Performance Task:
How Did the Author Show That Mr. Fox Was Smart?

Background

Mr. Fox did many things in the book, *Fantastic Mr. Fox*. The author, Roald Dahl, tried to make Mr. Fox seem to be a smart fox. What did Roald Dahl do to show that Mr. Fox was smart?

Task

Your job is to draw a picture that shows what you think the author did to show that Mr. Fox was smart.

Audience

The school library/media center teacher is making posters advertising the work of several authors. This picture is for the poster about Roald Dahl. Other students in the school will see this poster.

Purpose

The purpose of your drawing is to get other students interested in reading books by Roald Dahl.

Procedure

1. Review the assessment list for this task.
2. Make several small sketches of ideas for your picture.
3. Select one idea.
4. Create a full-page drawing that shows your idea about what Roald Dahl did to show that Mr. Fox was smart.
5. Use the assessment list to assess your work before you turn it in.
6. Turn in your work along with the assessment list showing your self-assessment.

Figure 4.14. Performance Task Assessment List: How Did the Author Show That Mr. Fox Was Smart?

Item	Assessment Points Possible	Points Earned Assessed by Self	Assessed by Teacher
1. Does my drawing show how the author told me that Mr. Fox was smart?	15	_____	_____
2. Did I use details in my drawing?	12	_____	_____
3. Did I use color to emphasize what Mr. Fox did?	6	_____	_____
4. Did I use proportion correctly?	6	_____	_____
5. Did I use foreground, middleground, and background in my drawing?	3	_____	_____
6. Does my drawing fill the page?	3	_____	_____
7. Is my work neat?	3	_____	_____
Total	**48**	_____	_____

Figure 4.15. Performance Task: Family Love

Background

In the book, *Go Fish*, Thomas and his Grandfather loved each other. What did Grandfather do to show his love for Thomas?

Task

Your job is to draw a picture that shows what Grandfather did to show his love for Thomas.

Audience

The school guidance counselor is displaying pictures of the ways family members show love for each other. You will give your picture to the guidance counselor.

Purpose

The purpose of your drawing is to teach other students and their family members about how family members can show love for one another.

Procedure

1. Review the assessment list for this task.
2. Make several small sketches of ideas for your picture.
3. Select one idea.
4. Create a full-page drawing that shows your idea about what Grandfather did to show his love for Thomas.
5. Use the assessment list to assess your work before you turn it in.
6. Turn in your work along with the assessment list showing your self-assessment.

Note to the teacher:

There is no assessment list provided for this task. Work with the class to create an assessment list.

The Performance Task Is One Part of a Unit of Instruction

The performance task is one activity in a unit often placed near, or at, the end of the unit to provide the students an opportunity to construct a response based on what they have learned throughout the entire unit. The unit may last two or three weeks, and the performance task lasts only one to two periods.

Whole Class Group, Group Work, and Individual Work

The unit of instruction may include various opportunities for whole class discussion, pair-shares and other forms of cooperative groups. When the performance task is introduced, it is usually an individual task so that each student can construct his own response, and the teacher can better understand what each individual knows and can show.

When the Performance Task Begins

Each student gets a copy of the assessment list, which is studied before the task begins, is referred to during the task, and is used for self-assessment at the end of the work. Note that in the Procedure for each performance task, the first step is to review the assessment list. and the last step is to use the assessment list for self-assessment.

While the Students Are Drawing

(In this chapter, all performance tasks ask for drawings as final products. In subsequent chapters, drawing is a pre-writing activity.)

♦ The teacher carries a copy of the assessment list as she or he walks around the room to see that all students are engaged.

♦ If a student is off task, talk with the student to clarify the task and then give the student a choice as to continue with the work (drawing in this case) or start over.

♦ As needed, talk with a student about one item on the assessment list. Focus the students on the specific part of their work relevant to the item on the assessment list in question.

♦ For the students who finish first, ask them to look at their work in relation to one item on the assessment list specified by the teacher. The teacher selects the item based on what they see in the student's work.

When the Drawings Are Finished, but before the Oral Presentations

- When the students are inexperienced using assessment lists, the teacher guides the class in looking at one item on the assessment list at a time. The teacher reads the assessment list item and asks the students to look at their own work and make a decision as to whether it is Terrific, Okay, or Needs Work. If the work is Terrific, the student gives himself all the points possible; if the work is Okay, the student gives himself the appropriate number of points for that level of quality. If the work is at the Needs Work level, the student gives himself that number of points.
- Finish the list, one item at a time.
- When students are more experienced with the assessment list, they can begin self-assessment on their own when they finish their work.
- The assessment lists are submitted with the final work.
- Do not start the oral presentations on the same day.

The Oral Presentations

- Each student brings their drawing back to the whole-class group meeting.
- The assessment list for the oral presentation is a poster format large enough for all to see.
- The teacher reads each item on the assessment list, and the class discusses what it means. The teacher may ask students to model certain behaviors, such as using a loud, large group voice.
- The teacher restates the task, e.g., "Show your drawing and explain how Roald Dahl showed that Mr. Fox was smart."
- Each student presents their drawing and gives the explanation.
- Assessment is not done on each individual student, but could be.
- Assessment is done after every one is finished presenting and explaining their drawing.
- An assessment list for oral presentations can focus on using a loud, sharing voice, staying on the topic, providing three examples, or using descriptive language.
- The teacher leads a discussion with the whole class as to how "we" did on each item on the assessment list. Item-by-item, the class decides if "we" were Terrific, Okay, or Needs Work.
- The teacher leads a discussion on what we could do better next time.
- The students turn it their drawings.

Final Steps

- The teacher reviews the student individual drawing and self-assessment.

- The teacher writes comments next to each item on each assessment list as to whether the teacher agrees with the self-assessment. When there is agreement, the teacher might write, "I agree." When there is a difference of opinion between the student and the teacher on an item in the assessment list, the teacher might write, "I disagree." The teacher also says why.

- The teacher decides which students need individual discussions regarding specific elements on their assessment lists.

- As needed, and on an individual basis, the teacher talks with the students to help them pick one way to improve their work. This process must be supportive, positive, and sensitive to the developmental level of students.

- If the task was an authentic performance task, the student's work is sent to its intended audience.

- Plan the next steps. Here the teacher reflects on the strengths, and this may include changing the wording of assessment list items. For example, item six in the assessment list in Figure 4.12 asks, "Did I use strong, bold colors to emphasize the actions of the dragon?" The next assessment list for a drawing might reword this statement to become, "Did I use colors to show how character X was brave?" Here the teacher would have decided that the students knew that the phrase "use colors" means "use strong, bold colors," and that the revised assessment list item was helping to make the students more responsible and independent in understanding what was expected of them.

  Later on, assessment lists for drawings might address the issue of using color by stating, "Did I use color well?" The teacher decides how quickly to revise assessment list items from very specific and explicit statements to more general statements.

Glossary of Terms

Item: An item in an analytic rubric or an assessment list.

Performance Task: A performance task is both a learning activity and an opportunity to assess student performance. In the area of reading comprehension, a performance task asks the student to do something such as describe and sequence (Initial Understanding), make and support inferences (Developing an Interpretation), compare and contrast (Making Connections), and judge and evaluate (Critical Stance.) In the primary grades, a performance task is limited to one such task.

Authentic Performance Task: When the work the students do during a performance task is intended to be for an audience outside of the classroom, such as the school principal, a parent, or grandparent, a student in another school, the mayor, or an author, the performance task is said to be authentic. Students are doing work that is just like work in the larger world.

Simulated Authentic Performance Task: When the task is not going to an intended audience, then the performance task is a simulated authentic performance task. The students may be pretending to write to the President, a Disney Studios movie director, George Washington, or a character in a book during a simulated authentic performance task. Both authentic and simulated authentic performance tasks put the student in the role of communicating with a person other than the classroom teacher or fellow classmates.

Looking-Ahead Planning: This is a strategy of selecting the performance task to be used in a unit of instruction well in advance of getting into a unit. Once the performance task has been selected, the teacher studies the task and its assessment list to focus on the content and process skills important to the students' success. The teacher pays particular attention to the challenging aspects of the new task and its assessment list, and then plans instruction to teach the important content and/or process skills.

References

Cameron, A. (1986). *More Stories Julian Tells* (A. Strugnell, Illus.). New York: Alfred A. Knopf

Dahl, R. (1961). *James and the Giant Peach* (N. E. Burkert, Illus.). New York: Bantam Skylark.

Dahl, R. (1970). *Fantastic Mr. Fox* (D. Chaffin, Illus.). New York: Bantam Skylark.

Gannett, R. S. (1948). *My Father's Dragon*. New York: Random House.

Koller , J. F. (1995). *The Fragonling. New York: Simon & Schuster*.

Schindler, S. D. (1985). *Every Living Thing*. New York: Simon & Schuster.

Steig, W. (1976). *Abel's Island*. Toronto: Collins.

Stolz, M. (1991). *Go Fish* (P. Cummings, Illus.). New York: HarperCollins.

5

Teaching and Assessing Reading Comprehension of Nonfiction through Drawing

Topics in This Chapter

♦ Strategies for using a framework for reading comprehension to plan performance tasks for nonfiction texts.

♦ Strategies to make holistic rubrics to use in conjunction with analytic rubrics and assessment lists.

♦ Strategies to use performance tasks and assessment tools in the context of social studies, science, and other disciplines using nonfiction texts.

Note: A glossary of terms is at the end of this chapter.

Four Levels of Comprehension

The four levels of comprehension are: Initial Understanding, Developing an Interpretation, Making Connections, and Critical Stance. These are defined in Chapter 3.

A list of some verbs used with each of these levels is presented in Figure 3.2.

Attention to Detail Through Drawing

The accurate reporting of showing detail through drawing is a form of Initial Understanding. When students are asked to "draw a picture of a cat skeleton" they may not pay attention to detail. But when the assignment is to pay attention to the details of the bones in a cat's jaws and teeth, and the preceding lessons have shown what it looks like when drawings show detail, the student's attention and drawings are much more precise. This attention to detail is the basis for the other levels of understanding that require the student to carry out such processes as inferring, comparing, contrasting, categorizing, or evaluating.

During a unit on Skeletons, to show **Initial Understanding**, a student may be asked to **illustrate** a cat's skull and describe the cat's jaws and teeth. To show **Developing an Interpretation**, the student may be asked to **explain** how the shape of the jaws and teeth help the cat catch and eat its food. To show **Making Connections**, the student may be asked to **compare** the jaws and teeth of a cat to those of a horse, and to **explain** how the shape of the bones helps each animal eat their food. To show **Critical Stance**, the student may be asked to **judge** which picture of a skeleton in the book is the best one to teach about bones. A unit on the skeleton would involve students in all four levels of comprehension. One particular performance task would engage students in only one or two of the levels of comprehension. It would take a series of tasks to cover all four levels of comprehension.

Attention to detail is a common shortcoming of students' writing. Main ideas may be presented, but often there are not enough supporting details. Drawing is a way to help many students pay attention to detail and, therefore, can be an effective pre-writing activity.

Principles and Elements of Design

The Principles and Elements of Design are presented and defined in Chapter 4. Figure 4.1 presents a chart used to plan which principles and elements will be used in specific performance tasks requiring students to make drawings. Collaboration with the art teacher is helpful in this process.

Drawings for the tasks about skeletons in this chapter require the student to draw accurate patterns of the bones and the unity of the whole skeleton. "Pattern," "shape," and "unity" are three important principles of design that are emphasized when tasks require the drawing of skeletons. Tasks about drawing skeletons would emphasize accurate use of shapes to show the pattern of bones in the whole skeleton. Likewise, the drawings of plants and simple machines in this chapter make use of pattern, and unity.

Rubrics for Drawings and Oral Presentations

Analytic Rubric for Drawing and Oral Presentations

The analytic rubrics for drawings and oral presentations are presented in Chapter 4, Figures 4.2 and 4.3.

Holistic Rubrics for Drawings and Oral Presentations

Figures 5.1 and 5.2 present holistic rubrics for drawings and oral presentations.

A holistic rubric is used to describe the overall quality of a student's work or performance. For example, the holistic rubric for a drawing addresses the same traits addressed by the analytic rubric for the drawing. Whereas the analytic rubric provides details of quality for each trait, the holistic rubric just gives a "big picture" for the overall quality of the student's work. The holistic rubrics in this chapter show four levels of performance: "Above Goal," "At Goal," "Near Goal," and "Below Goal." The "Goal" refers to the level of performance that the classroom teacher, school or school district sets as the standard to meet. If you were to assign a "report card grade" to the level titled "At Goal" it would be about a B or B+. Work better than that is "Above Goal," work almost as good as "At Goal" is called "Near Goal," and work very inferior to "At Goal" is called "Below Goal."

It is essential that examples of student work be selected that show what it "looks like or sounds like" "Above Goal," "At Goal," "Near Goal," and "Below Goal." The holistic rubric and the examples of student work together define what is meant by the four levels of performance. Models of excellent drawings would be the drawings themselves. Models of excellent oral presentations would be oral presentations on video tapes.

The teacher can use the holistic rubric within a grade to track the progress towards, and even beyond, the goal. "At Goal" drawings and oral presentations in grade one would be of less quality than "At Goal" work in an upper grade. The same holistic rubric can be used for a sequence of grade levels, but the student work serving as examples for each of the levels within the holistic rubric must be appropriate to each grade level in that sequence. A student "At Goal" in grade three and still "At Goal" in grade five would have made much progress because the standards of excellence to be "At Goal" in grade five are much higher than in grade three.

One problem with holistic rubrics is that they may not be able to show specifically why a student is overall "Near Goal." There are many reasons that the student's work may be described as only "Near Goal." For example, the work of one student may be Near Goal because proportions are not used well enough, whereas the work of another student may be Near Goal because foreground, middleground, and background are not used well enough. The holistic "score" does not give the teacher or student precise information about specific strengths and needs of individual students. The use of rubrics to help generate assessment lists is discussed later in this chapter.

Figure 5.1. Holistic Rubric for Drawings

Level of Performance	Description of the Level of Performance
Above Goal	The student's drawing is completely on the topic of the assignment and uses many accurate details. The student also uses proportion very accurately; uses foreground, middleground, and background well (if needed), uses the elements of design very well as called for in the assignment, uses all of the paper, and is very neat.
At Goal	The student's drawing is on the topic of the assignment and uses several accurate details. The student uses most of the following areas such as: uses proportion mostly accurately; uses foreground, middleground, and background (if needed), uses the elements of design well as called for in the assignment, uses most of the paper, and is neat.
Near Goal	The student's drawing is mostly on the topic and uses a few accurate details. There is a significant shortcoming in two or more areas such as: use of proportion; use of foreground, middleground, and background; or the elements of design required by the assignment.
Below Goal	The student's drawing is not on the topic and/or uses inaccurate details. There are many shortcomings in areas such as the use of proportion, the elements of design, use of paper space, and neatness.

Figure 5.2. Holistic Rubric for Oral Presentations

Level of Performance	Description of the Level of Performance
Above Goal	The student displays the drawing very clearly to everyone and as often as necessary. The student uses a loud, group-sharing voice throughout the presentation. The student provides accurate, detailed information on the topic and according to the thinking-skill verb for this task, i.e., the student provides information to both compare and contrast if the task calls for those thinking skills. The student uses excellent descriptive language and vocabulary appropriate to the topic.
At Goal	The student displays the drawing clearly to everyone. The student uses a loud, group-sharing voice most of the time in the presentation. The student provides accurate information on the topic and according to the thinking-skill verb for this task, i.e., the student provides information to both compare and contrast if the task calls for those thinking skills. The level of detail is satisfactory but not at the excellent level. The student uses descriptive language and some vocabulary appropriate to the topic.
Near Goal	The student does not display the drawing clearly enough. The student's voice is too soft. The student provides some information on the topic but some may be inaccurate, i.e., the task may require three details and the student only provides one or supplies three and one is inaccurate. The student does not completely respond to the requirement of the thinking-skill verb, i.e., the student provides information about the similarities of two things when the thinking skill calls for both similarities and differences. The student uses little descriptive language and/or vocabulary specific to the topic.
Below Goal	The student displays the drawing poorly and uses a voice that is much too soft. The information in the presentation is off topic, inaccurate, and/or insufficient in quantity. The student does not provide information according to the thinking-skill verb, i.e., the student may only describe one element rather than comparing and contrasting it with another element.

Making Performance Tasks

Drawing provides the information needed in the oral presentation. When the overall task is to describe, the drawing presents the information that the student points to during the oral description. Likewise, if the overall task is to compare two skulls, the drawing provides the accurate details and the comparison is made in the oral presentation. The tasks in this chapter require both drawing and oral presentation as final products of their work. In the book, *Assessing and Teaching Reading Comprehension and Writing, Grades 3–5* (Vol. 4), drawing and writing are the initial, pre-writing steps that lead to various types of written final products.

Developing Ideas for Performance Tasks

Making a chart of ideas helps ensure that the overall collection of performance tasks addresses all four levels of comprehension. Figure 5.3 presents tasks for each of the topics of water, skeletons, and machines.

Creating a chart of ideas for performance tasks in each of the four levels of comprehension also helps avoid two common problems of creating sets of performance tasks. The first problem is the tendency to make too many tasks at the Initial Understanding level. The second problem is to have too few tasks at the Critical Stance level. A balance of all four levels is desirable.

Creating the Performance Task

Once ideas have been generated for performance tasks, they can be engineered into actual performance tasks for students. Consider the idea for the performance task that states, "Draw and label a picture of the skull of a cat emphasizing the structure of the cat's jaws and teeth." This is an "Initial Understanding" task because the student is being asked to simply draw and label the structures. When the task is reworded to read, "Draw and label a picture that shows how the jaws and teeth of a cat help it catch and eat its food," then the task becomes a "Developing an Interpretation" task.

Figure 5.4 (page 91) presents the final version of a completed performance task. The following comments explain how this task is constructed to have a Background, Task, Audience, Purpose, and Procedure.

- All of the narrative in the task is written "**to the student**."
- The **Background** sets the stage for the task. In this task, the students are reminded that they have learned about the Water Cycle and that a first-grade teacher needs some pictures of the Water Cycle to help her teach the Water Cycle to her students. The Background is kept short.

Figure 5.3. Menu of Ideas for Performance Tasks

| Book Title | Levels of Comprehension | | | |
	Initial Understanding	Developing an Interpretation	Making Connections	Critical Stance
• *Pond and River* (plus hands-on activities and a field trip to a river and pond)	Draw and label a picture of one insect, one amphibian, one reptile, one fish, one bird, and one mammal that live in the water of a pond or river. (list)	Draw and label a picture of the food chain in a pond to show what eats what. (describe relationships)	Draw and label a picture comparing and contrasting a water plant with a plant that grows in a field. (compare and contrast)	Draw and label one more picture that should be included in this book. (extend)
• *Rivers and Lakes*	Draw and label a picture of the water cycle that includes a river or a lake. (describe)	Draw and label a picture that shows how much power a river has to have to change land. (interpret)	On one piece of paper, draw and label four pictures that show four different ways that rivers are important to people. (generalize)	Draw and label a picture of especially interesting information about water in this book. (evaluate)
• *Cat* • *Horse* • *Skeleton* • *Skeletons*	Draw and label a picture of the skull of an animal in the cat family. (describe)	Draw and label a picture that shows how the jaws and teeth of an animal in the cat family help it catch and eat its food. (explain)	Draw and label pictures that show the similarities and differences between the jaws and teeth of a cat and the jaws and teeth of a horse? (compare and contrast)	Add a chapter to the Eyewitness Book on Skeletons about an imaginary animal that eats turtles. Draw and label one picture of the skull of that imaginary animal. (extend)
• *Simple Machines* • *Levers* • *Inclined Planes* • *Wheels* • *The New Way Things Work*	Draw and label pictures of four different simple machines. (identify)	Draw and label a picture of one simple machine that is most important to you. (defend)	Illustrate how you would use simple machines to design a complex machine to weigh an elephant. (design, integrate)	Select one picture or drawing that was confusing to you. Draw a picture that makes that picture or drawing easier to understand. (identify error)

- The **Task** tells the student exactly what he is to make or do in the performance task. In this case, the student is to draw and label a picture of the Water Cycle.

- The section of the task entitled, "**Audience**," explains for whom the work is intended. This task identifies first graders as the audience. Other tasks in this chapter use peers, engineers at a university, and parents. Authentic tasks have real audiences, wheres simulated authentic tasks have simulated audiences.

- The section of the task entitled, "**Purpose**" explains why the student is doing this work for the specified audience. In this case, the purpose of the student's work is to teach the first graders about the Water Cycle. The "Purpose" is the "intended impact" the student's work is to have on the audience.

- The **Procedure** presents a short, simple list of the steps in the performance task. The assessment lists will focus the students on how to pay attention to the quality of their work. The Procedure is like a checklist of what to do, and the assessment list addresses the quality of the work.

- The whole performance task is no longer than one page.

Making Assessment Lists for the Performance Tasks

The teacher who is creating an assessment list for a performance task that asks students to make a drawing refers to the analytic and holistic rubrics for drawings for ideas. For example, the items of the resulting assessment list are worded to be well-connected to the content of the performance task. The first two items in the analytic rubric in Figure 4.2 (page 55) address the content and details necessary for a drawing. In the assessment list shown in Figure 5.8 (page 95), items one and two are specifically connected to the content of the picture.

The following are some guidelines for making assessment lists for specific performance tasks. The guidelines for creating performance tasks presented in Chapter 4 are summarized here:

- **The purpose of an assessment list is to get the students to pay attention to the details of their work**. Therefore, the number of items and the wording of each item must be appropriate to this purpose. The assessment list in Figure 5.8 has seven items and the assessment list in Figure 5.10 (page 97) has 13 items. Teachers put only as many items into an assessment list as students will pay attention to.

- **Make sure that some items are clearly related to the content of the performance task.** Items one and two in Figure 5.8 show that the content of the task is to show the relationship between the structures of the jaw and teeth of a cat and the functions of catching and eating.

- **Create some items about the use of process skills**. Items four through eight in Figure 5.5 focus on the process skills involved in making realistic drawings from observations.

- **Create some "Sure Thing" items** that must be about what the students will find easy to do because of their knowledge and skills. Item three in Figure 5.8 asks the students to use details in the drawings. The teacher who used this assessment list knew that her students were good at including details, so she included this item to reinforce that skill.

- **Create one or two "Challenge" items** that should be a challenge for the students, i.e., something that students will find more difficult to do. Some instruction before the task begins will focus on " Challenge" areas. Items five and six in Figure 5.8 were included by the teacher because she knew her students were still having difficulty drawing things using correct shape and proportion. She included these two items to focus her teaching and the students' learning on using shape and proportion correctly.

- **Adjust the specificity of items**. Challenge items must be stated in very detailed and specific terms. Item six in Figure 5.5 (page 92) asks, "Did I use color to emphasize the events in the Water Cycle?" This question is more specific than asking, "Did I use color to emphasize what happened?" or "Did I use color well?" The teacher decides how specific to make the item. Inexperienced students need very specific items. As the students get more experience, more responsibility should be placed on them to "understand" what an assessment list item means.

When an experienced student reads the assessment list item, "Did I use color well?," he expands that statement in his head to become, "Did I use the appropriate colors in the right intensity to emphasize the particular part of the picture that I want to stand out to my audience?" The long-term goal of using assessment lists is to help students create assessment lists in their heads and to no longer need assessment lists from teachers. That long-term goal can be met after years of experience with assessment lists.

- **Adjust the complexity of items**. A simple item in an assessment list involves only one direction, and a complex item involves two or more. Items one through six in Figure 5.10 each focus on a different aspect of the drawing . Keeping the items simple like this may mean that the assessment list is longer. But, simplicity is important for students learning to use assessment lists. When students are more experienced, the item in the assessment list might read, "Did I use at least one wheel, pulley, level, inclined plain, and spring?"

♦ **Put items in question format**. Questions invite and encourage active learning.

♦ **Involve students in helping to create assessment lists**. The point of assessment lists is to coach students to take responsibility for assessing and improving their own work. When possible, the students should be involved in conversations to create assessment lists.

After the students are experienced in using several assessment lists, for example, making drawings of skeletons, the teacher might work with the whole group to create an assessment list for the drawing of plants required in the next performance task.

Assessment Lists for Drawings and for Oral Descriptions of Drawings

Each task in this chapter includes an assessment list for the student's drawing. Several of the performance tasks in this chapter also have assessment lists for oral presentations. An alternative for an assessment list handout for an oral presentation is an assessment list on a large poster displayed in the room and used when necessary.

Using Performance Tasks and Assessment Lists

Chapter 4 presents information on how to use assessment lists with students. Two points to revisit are:

1. Keep the performance tasks short—one or two class periods. The performance task is not a "unit of instruction"; it is one component in that unit.
2. Although various forms of group work may be included in the unit, the performance task is almost always individual work.

Figure 5.4. Performance Task: The Water Cycle

Background

Water is essential to all living things. Without water we would die. The way water moves through the environment is called the "Water Cycle." First-grade children are studying the Water Cycle, and their teacher needs your help.

Task

Your job is to draw and label a picture of the Water Cycle to give to this first-grade teacher.

Audience

The audience for your picture will be the first-grade children.

Purpose

The purpose of your picture is to teach the first-grade children about the Water Cycle.

Procedure

1. Review the assessment list for this drawing.
2. Sketch the water cycle you will draw.
3. Draw and label the water cycle.
4. Use the assessment list to assess your own work.
5. Turn in your work and your self-assessment to your teacher.

Figure 5.5. Performance Task Assessment List: The Water Cycle

| | | | Points Earned | |
	Item	Assessment Points Possible	Assessed by Self	Assessed by Teacher
1.	Does my drawing show at least three parts of the Water Cycle?	15	_____	_____
2.	Did I include a lake or river in my drawing?	6	_____	_____
3.	Does my drawing show how the parts of the Water Cycle are a "circle of events?"	15	_____	_____
4.	Did I label each part correctly?	6	_____	_____
5.	Did I use arrows with my labels?	3	_____	_____
6.	Did I use color to emphasize the events in the Water Cycle?	6	_____	_____
7.	Did I use the full space of my paper for my drawing?	3	_____	_____
8.	Is my work neat?	3	_____	_____
	Total	57	_____	_____

For item 1, Terrific work gets a score of 15, Okay work gets a score of 10; and Needs Work ges a score no greater than 5.

Figure 5.6. Performance Task Assessment List:
Oral Presentation of the Drawing of the Water Cycle

| | | Points Earned | |
	Assessment Points Possible	Assessed by Self	Assessed by Teacher
Item			
1. Did I hold my drawing so that everyone could see it?	6	_____	_____
2. Did I use a loud, group-sharing voice?	12	_____	_____
3. Did I look at my audience enough?	3	_____	_____
4. Did I describe all the parts of the Water Cycle in my drawing?	15	_____	_____
5. Did I include details in my descriptions?	12	_____	_____
6. Did I stay on the topic?	6	_____	_____
Total	54	_____	_____

Figure 5.7. Performance Task:
Jaws of the Jungle

Background

All living things must have food to stay alive. Mammals have jaws and teeth that are designed to help them catch and eat their food.

Task

Your task is to draw and label the skull of a member of the cat family to show the details of how its jaws and teeth help it catch and eat its food.

Audience

Your pictures will be displayed in the library near the books about skeletons. The audience for your drawing is the other students in your school.

Purpose

One purpose of your drawings is to teach other students about how the structure of an animal's jaws and teeth are related to the food it eats. Another purpose of your drawing is to interest other students in reading library books about skeletons.

Procedure

1. Review the assessment list for this drawing.
2. Sketch how you will show the jaws and teeth of the animal.
3. Make the final drawing and label the parts.
4. Use the assessment list to self-assess.
5. Turn in your work with your self-assessment to your teacher.

Figure 5.8. Performance Task Assessment List: Jaws of the Jungle

	Item	Assessment Points Possible	Points Earned	
			Assessed by Self	Assessed by Teacher
1.	Does my drawing show the jaws and teeth of the cat I selected?	12	_____	_____
2.	Does my drawing show exactly how the shape of the jaws and teeth help the cat to catch and eat its food?	24	_____	_____
3.	Did I use details?	12	_____	_____
4.	Did I label the parts correctly?	12	_____	_____
5.	Did I use shape correctly?	12	_____	_____
6.	Did I use proportion correctly?	6	_____	_____
7.	Is my work neat?	6	_____	_____
	Total	84	_____	_____

Figure 5.9. Performance Task: How to Weigh an Elephant

Background

Machines help us make our work easier. Engineers invent machines to solve problems. How would you invent a machine to weigh an elephant?

Task

Your task is to invent a complex machine using at least one wheel, one level, one pulley, one inclined plane, and one spring to weigh a real elephant.

Audience

The engineers at the university are interested in how elementary-school students can make inventions based on simple machines. Your pictures will be sent to the engineers.

Purpose

The purpose of your drawings of your inventions is to impress the engineers.

Procedure

1. Review the assessment list for this drawing.
2. Sketch the invention using all the required parts.
3. Draw and label the invention.
4. Use the assessment list to self-assess.
5. Turn in your work with your self-assessment to your teacher.

Figure 5.10. Performance Task Assessment List: How to Weigh an Elephant

Item	Assessment Points Possible	Points Earned	
		Assessed by Self	Assessed by Teacher
1. Did I use at least one wheel?	6	_____	_____
2. Did I use at least one pulley?	6	_____	_____
3. Did I use at least one level?	6	_____	_____
4. Did I use at least one inclined plane?	6	_____	_____
5. Did I use at least one spring?	6	_____	_____
6. Did I include the elephant in my drawing?	6	_____	_____
7. Do all the parts of my machine work together to do the job of weighing a real elephant?	30	_____	_____
8. Did I show details?	12	_____	_____
9. Did I label all the parts?	12	_____	_____
10. Did I add labels that show how the parts work?	12	_____	_____
11. Did I use shapes correctly?	12	_____	_____
12. Did I use proportion correctly?	12	_____	_____
13. Is my work neat?	12	_____	_____
Total	**138**	_____	_____

Figure 5.11. Performance Task Assessment List: Oral Presentation for How to Weigh an Elephant

	Item	Assessment Points Possible	Points Earned Assessed by Self	Points Earned Assessed by Teacher
1.	Did I hold the picture of my drawing so that everyone in the class could see it clearly?	6	_____	_____
2.	Did I use my loud, group-sharing voice?	6	_____	_____
3.	Did I point out each simple machine? • Wheel • Pulley • Lever • Inclined Plane • Spring	15	_____	_____
4.	Did I describe how they are all put together to make a complex machine?	15	_____	_____
5.	Did I describe the details of how the machine works to weigh an elephant?	15	_____	_____
6.	Did I stay on the topic?	6	_____	_____
	Total	63	_____	_____

Figure 5.12. Performance Task:
Turtle Eater

Background

The *Eyewitness Book, Skeleton*, has 64 chapters including the glossary of bone names. Each chapter taught you more about skeletons. Pretend that you are the illustrator. Illustrate a new chapter about an imaginary animal that eats hard-shelled turtles.

Task

Your task is to draw the skull of this imaginary animal and show how its jaws and teeth help it catch and eat the hard-shelled turtles.

Audience

Your school is creating an imaginary zoo for open house and your pictures will be part of that display.

Purpose

The purpose of your drawing is to entertain the parents at open house and to teach them about how the jaws and teeth of animals help them catch and eat their food.

Procedure

1. Review the assessment list for this drawing.
2. Sketch the skull you will draw.
3. Draw and label the skull.
4. Use the assessment list to self-assess.
5. Turn in your work with your self-assessment to your teacher.

Figure 5.13. Performance Task Assessment List:
Turtle Eater

Item	Assessment Points Possible	Points Earned	
		Assessed by Self	Assessed by Teacher
1. Does my drawing show the skull of the Turtle Eater?	12	_____	_____
2. Did I show how the structure of the jaws and teeth of the Turtle Eater help it catch and eat its food?	30	_____	_____
3. Did I label the parts and how they work?	12	_____	_____
4. Did I use details?	15	_____	_____
5. Did I use shape correctly?	15	_____	_____
6. Did I use proportion correctly?	12	_____	_____
7. Is my work neat?	12	_____	_____
Total	**108**	_____	_____

Glossary of Terms

Holistic Rubric: This type of scoring tool looks at the overall performance and gives it a rating. Whereas an analytic rubric rates a number of separate skills or aspects of a student's work, the holistic rubric looks at the "big picture" of the student's work and gives it an overall rating. The rating can be over a six-, five-, four-, or even three-level range. The holistic rubrics in this book are based on a four-level scale: Above Goal, At Goal, Near Goal, and Below Goal. Student work at the "At Goal" level represents the high standards sought.

References

Water

Levete, S. (1999). *Rivers and Lakes*. Brookfield, CT: Copper Beech Books.

Pounds, E. T. (1974). *Once There Was a River: A Story of Water Pollution*. New York: Scott, Foresman.

Skeletons

Clutton-Brock, J. (1991). *Cats*. New York: Alfred A. Knopf.

Clutton-Brock, J. (1992). *Horses*. New York: Alfred A. Knopf.

Johnson, J. (1994). *Skeletons* (E. Gray, Illus). Pleasantville, NY: Reader's Digest.

Parker, S. (1988). *Skeleton*. New York: Alfred A. Knopf.

Machines

Lampton, C. (1991). *Bathtubs Slides Roller Coaster Rails: Simple Machines that are Really Inclined Planes* (C. Nicklaus, Illus.). Brookfield, CT: Millbrook Press.

Lampton, C. (1991). *Marbles Roller Skates Doorknobs: Simple Machines that are Really Wheels* (C. Nicklaus, Illus.). Brookfield, CT: Millbrook Press.

Lampton, C. (1991). *Sailboats Flagpoles Cranes: Using Pulleys as Simple Machines* (C. Nicklaus, Illus.). Brookfield, CT: Millbrook Pres.

Lampton, C. (1991). *Seesaws Nutcrackers Brooms: Simple Machines that are Really Levers* (C. Nicklaus, Illus.). Brookfield, CT: Millbrook Press.

Macaulay, D. (1988). *The New Way Things Work*. Boston: Houghton Mifflin.

6

Teaching and Assessing Reading Comprehension through the Use of Graphic Organizers

Topics in This Chapter

- ♦ Strategies for using graphic organizers to help students process information according to the thinking-skill verb used in the task.
- ♦ Strategies to create performance tasks that use graphic organizers and oral presentation.
- ♦ Strategies to create assessment tools to assess the quality of student's use of graphic organizers.
- ♦ Strategies to base grades for report cards on assessments.

Note: The graphic organizers referred to in this chapter are in Appendix A.

Graphic Organizers

A graphic organizer is a diagram that represents a relationship directed by a thinking-skill verb. The verb "**sequence**" calls for a diagram of a series of boxes connected by arrows that shows the "event" of one box leading to the "event" of another box. The sequence could be the events in the story. The verb "**compare**" could be supported by a diagram with two side-by-side boxes. The characteristics of one thing would be listed in one box and the characteristics of the other thing would be listed in the second box. There are many types of graphic organizers that could be used to help the student organize information to make a comparison.

The purpose of a graphic organizer is to give the student support in processing information according to the thinking-skill verb in the performance task. When the student sees that the task calls for sequencing, describing, inferring, predicting, comparing, or rating, the student should eventually be able to process information on his own without the help of a graphic organizer. But while students are gaining experience in processing information, the graphic organizer is a guide.

Figure 6.1 presents the sequence of events in using graphic organizers. Notice that the sequence is in the form of a cycle. Steps A through F constitute a cycle of identifying the thinking-skill verb, getting a graphic organizer to use, using the graphic organizer to process information, assessing the quality of the work, reflecting on strengths and needs, planning for improvement, and then starting the cycle over again.

Figure 6.1 also shows a second sequence represented by steps 1 to 3. This sequence represents the work teachers do over several years, i.e., grades K–5, to coach students to be independent learners making decisions about selecting, creating, and using graphic organizers to support their thinking.

As the students gain proficiency in using teacher-selected graphic organizers, they progress to selecting the graphic organizer to use from a wall poster, and, finally, to creating their own.

The Connection between Thinking-Skill Verbs, Drawings, and Graphic Organizers

The previous two chapters ask students to draw pictures and then give oral explanations of what the pictures showed. These pre-writing strategies help students find, organize, and process information in preparation for writing.

Drawings ask students to arrange information "on the space" of the paper. Sequences of activities are drawn in sequence. A drawing of two characters, or a character and the student side-by-side, provides the opportunity for the student to compare and contrast. The visual organization of information supports the thinking skill important to the task.

A graphic organizer is another way to organize information "in space" to support a thinking skill. The graphic organizer requires the student to arrange words and simple phrases in the space of the graphic organizer. The physical act of putting the words or phrases "in space" supports the "pattern of thinking" required by the task.

The graphic organizers in this book, *Assessing and Teaching Reading Comprehension and Pre-Writing 3–5* (Vol. 3), help students gather, process, and organize information. Volume 4, *Assessing and Teaching Reading Comprehension and Writing 3–5* (Vol. 4), will use these graphic organizers to plan specific types of writing, such as stories, newspaper articles, and persuasive letters.

Figure 6.1. Using Graphic Organizers to Support Thinking

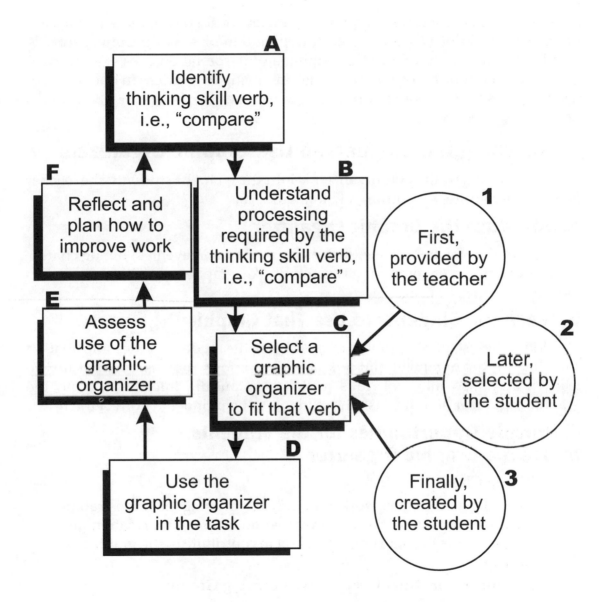

Selecting a Set of Graphic Organizers to Use During the Year

Figure 6.2 matches each graphic organizer in this chapter to one or more thinking-skill verbs. Each graphic organizer has a reference number in the lower left-hand corner. Some graphic organizers could be for a task at the comprehension level of Developing an Interpretation or Making Connections. A task involving the student in Developing an Interpretation uses one information source, i.e., one book, whereas a task involving the student in Making Connections uses two or more information sources, i.e., two books, or a book and a personal experience.

Teaching the Students to Use Graphic Organizers

Each time a new graphic organizer is introduced to the students, the teacher follows the five steps, A through E, in Figure 6.3.

A. Introduce the Graphic Organizer

Explain the task to be done, such as, sequencing an event, showing characteristics of a thing, or comparing two things. The graphic organizer helps us do the job.

B. Teach the Students to Use That Graphic Organizer

Model the use of the graphic organizer for the students. Place information into the graphic organizer and talk about the information as you add it. The teacher may also make obvious mistakes in putting information into the graphic organizer and then ask the students to help find and correct them.

C. Provide Opportunities for the Students to Use the Graphic Organizer

♦ **Whole Class**

Next, the teacher may work with the class in using the same graphic organizer for a new task. The teacher adds some information and asks students to come up to the easel to contribute to the graphic organizer.

♦ **Pair-Shares or Other Cooperative Learning Groups**

Then, the teacher may assign the task of using that same graphic organizer for a new task to a pair of students or a small group. For example, if the students as a whole class have learned to use graphic organizer GO1 (page 168) to sequence the events in a book the teacher has just read to the class, the pair or cooperative learning group would use that same graphic organizer to work on a new task asking them to sequence the events in another story.

Figure 6.2. Graphic Organizers and Thinking-Skill Verbs

IU = Initial Understanding DI = Developing an Interpretation		
MC = Making Connections CS = Critical Stance		
Graphic Organizer	*Level of Comprehension IU, DI, MC, CS*	*Thinking-Skill Verb(s) Used for This Graphic Organizer Include:*
GO1, GO2, GO3	IU	Sequence
GO4	IU	Sequence (cycle)
GO5	DI or MC	Hypothesize, Infer
GO6	DI or MC	Predict
GO7	DI or MC	Describe Relationship, Describe Cause and Effect, Interpret
GO8, GO9	DI or MC	Compare, Contrast, Categorize, Generalize
GO10	IU and DI or MC	Describe, Identify, Analyze, Explain
GO11, GO12, GO13, GO14, GO15	IU or DI or MC	List, Describe, Examine, Infer, Interpret, Summarize, Support
GO16	DI	Conclude, Draw Conclusions, Explain, Infer, Interpret, Summarize
GO17	DI or MC	Examine, Infer, Interpret, Summarize, Support
GO18, GO19, GO20, GO22	IU or DI or MC	Analyze, Conclude, Decide, Describe, Examine, Infer, Interpret, List, Predict, Summarize and others
GO21, GO23, GO24	CS	Assess, Evaluate, Judge, Rate

- **Colored Marker or Crayon Strategy**

  Contributing information to a graphic organizer is an excellent co-operative group learning activity. To assure that each student makes contributions, ask each student to use a different colored pen, marker, or crayon to record his information. The finished graphic organizer should show information in all the colors used by the group.

- **Individuals**

  Finally, when the teacher feels that the students have enough large- and small-group experience with that graphic organizer for skills such as sequencing, individual performance tasks requiring the use of that graphic organizer are used. Now, individual students are completing their own graphic organizer for sequencing the events in a story or a nonfiction text.

D. Guide the Students' Self-Assessment

The teacher models using an assessment list to assess work done in a graphic organizer during the teacher's original modeling. The same assessment list is used for the small-group work and then for the individual work. These assessment lists may contain only three to five elements.

E. Guide the Students' Self-Reflection and Goal Setting

At the end of a whole-group activity with the graphic organizer, the teacher asks, "How did we do? Terrific? Okay? Or Needs Work?" When a student volunteers a response, he is asked to explain. Then, the class talks about how to be better in using graphic organizers. The teacher talks to the pairs or small groups and engages them in the same assessment and goal setting. At this point, the teacher may introduce an assessment list that uses a point system, and may help the class and small groups to practice using it. Finally, individual students use the assessment lists with points with performance tasks that call for working in graphic organizers.

Encourage Students through Showing Off Their Terrific Work

When students do terrific work, e.g., get the highest number of points possible for an element in the assessment list, ask them to show it off, and then post it for a day in the classroom. Look for opportunities to acknowledge the terrific work of students who usually do not do terrific work. Refrain from using praise such as, "You are great at using graphic organizers." Rephrase your comments to be an encouragement by saying, "I like the way you have shown the details in your graphic organizer that sequence the exploration of Lewis and Clark."

Praise focuses on the student, and encouragement focuses on the student's work. Ultimately, encouragement is much more motivating to the student.

Continue the Cycle Each Time a New Graphic Organizer Is Introduced

Repeat the five steps each time a new graphic organizer is introduced. Add samples of student work to the Gallery of Excellence for each of the new graphic organizers. By the end of the year, two or three samples of student work will model the whole collection of graphic organizers learned that year.

Late in the year when the gallery presents several types of graphic organizers, the teacher may hold a whole-class meeting to discuss a new task such as sequencing the events in a new story or comparing animals from two different regions of the United States. As part of that discussion, the teacher may ask the students to suggest a type of graphic organizer to use for a specific task. Thus, the students are learning to be more independent in using graphic organizers. Ultimately, in the upper grades, students will be selecting and creating their own graphic organizers to help them in their projects.

Ask the Students to Help Select the Graphic Organizer to Use

If the teacher selects eight to ten graphic organizes on which to focus during the year, students can become so familiar with their use that they can work with the teacher to pick a graphic organizer for a new task. The set of graphic organizers that comprise the collection for the year can be posted in the room. Then, when an opportunity arises that calls for the use of a graphic organizer, the teacher can ask, "Which one of our graphic organizers should be used this time?" The teacher accepts suggestions and asks for explanations for why a specific suggestion was made. The teacher leads the group to a consensus, and that graphic organizer is used.

Figure 6.3. Teaching Students to Use Graphic Organizers

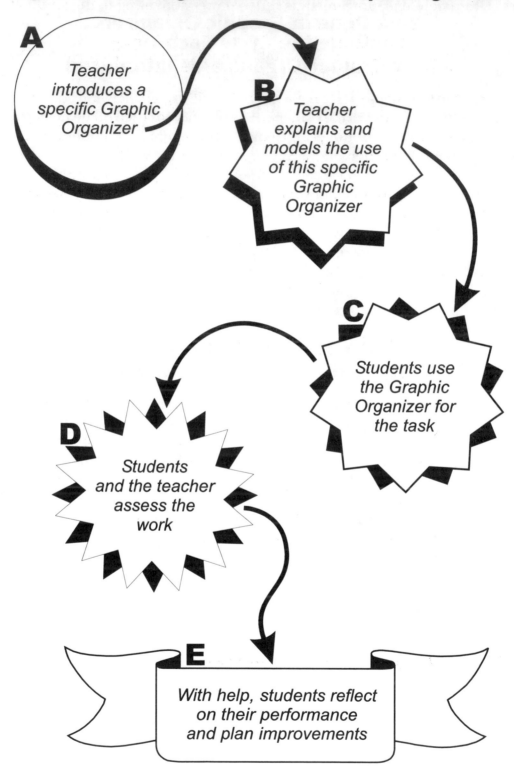

A Teacher introduces a specific Graphic Organizer

B Teacher explains and models the use of this specific Graphic Organizer

C Students use the Graphic Organizer for the task

D Students and the teacher assess the work

E With help, students reflect on their performance and plan improvements

Analytic and Holistic Rubrics for Work Done in Graphic Organizers

As with drawing and oral presentation, analytic and holistic rubrics can be used to assess student performance in putting information into graphic organizers. Creating these rubrics also provides ideas for creating assessment lists for performance tasks. The assessment lists are the tools to help students learn to pay attention to the quality of their work and improve their performance. The assessment lists help the teacher focus on specific aspects of the student's work. The holistic rubrics enable the teacher to give an overall rating to a student's work. The analytic rubric helps the teacher identify the specific strengths and weaknesses of student work so that subsequent instruction can reinforce strengths and improve deficits.

Figures 6.4 and 6.5 (pages 112, 113) present analytic rubrics for student work in graphic organizers and their oral description of their work. Each of these rubrics can be used for graphic organizers that call only for drawing, and graphic organizers that ask for drawing and writing, or only writing. Figures 6.6 and 6.7 present the respective holistic rubric counterparts of Figures 6.4 and 6.5.

Figure 6.4 shows that all the items in the analytic rubric for work completed in a graphic organizer are weighted equally, e.g., each item has the weight of "1." Another strategy would be to weight some items more than others because they may be more important. For example, the item, "Information Is Accurate," could be assigned the weight of "4." Then, a rating of "Terrific" on "Information Is Accurate" would be "12" (4 for Information Is Accurate x 3 for Traffic = 12.)

Figure 6.4. Analytic Rubric for Work Done in a Graphic Organizer

Element	Level of Performance		
	Above Goal Weight = 3	Goal Weight = 2	Needs Work Weight = 1
Information Is on the Topic Weight = 1	All of the information is on the topic.	Most of the information is on the topic.	Most of the information is off the topic.
Information Is Accurate Weight = 1	All the information is accurate.	Most of the information is accurate. No major errors are made.	Most of the information is incorrect.
Appropriate Amount of Information Is Provided Weight = 1	There are enough details without overdoing it.	There are a few too many or too few details.	There are too few details or no details.
Information Is in the Correct Spaces Weight = 1	All of the information in the graphic organizer is placed correctly.	Most of the information in the graphic organizer is placed correctly.	Many mistakes are made in placing information in the graphic organizer.
Vocabulary Weight = 1	Vocabulary related to the topic is especially well chosen.	Vocabulary of the topic is well-chosen.	Vocabulary of the topic is not well chosen.
Spelling Weight = 1	All spelling is correct.	High-frequency words are spelled correctly, and other words are spelled so they can be read.	Mistakes are made in high-frequency words and other words.
Neat and Presentable Weight = 1	The work is very neat and presentable.	The work is mostly neat and presentable.	The work is neither neat nor presentable.
Overall	Above Goal	Near Goal	Needs Work

Figure 6.5. Analytic Rubric for an Oral Presentation of Information in a Graphic Organizer

Element	Level of Performance		
	Above Goal **Weight = 3**	**Goal** **Weight = 2**	**Needs Work** **Weight = 1**
Presentation Follows the Pattern of the Graphic Organizer Weight = 1	The students oral presentation stays right with the pattern of the graphic organizer. For example, if the graphic organizer is about a comparison, the oral presentation makes that comparison and only that comparison.	The oral presentation sticks mostly with the purpose of the graphic organizer.	The student presents the information, but not in the pattern of the graphic organizer. For example, the student may present all of the information relevant to the "comparison" but the presentation does not actually make the comparison.
Presentation Includes Accurate Details Weight = 1	The student presents all of the details required.	The student presents most of the details required.	The student does not present enough details.
Vocabulary Weight = 1	The student uses all of the vocabulary required in the lesson.	The student uses most of the vocabulary required in the lesson.	The student does not use sufficient vocabulary.
Presentation Stays on the Topic Weight = 1	The presentation is entirely on the topic.	The presentation is mostly on the topic.	The presentation strays off the topic.
Uses Strong, Group-Sharing Voice Weight = 1	The student uses a good, strong, group-sharing voice throughout the presentation.	The student uses the strong, group-sharing voice for most of the presentation.	The student does not use a strong, group-sharing voice.
Overall	Above Goal	Goal	Needs Work

Note: Each element in this analytic rubric has been assigned the weight of "1." An alternative strategy would be to weight some elements more heavily than others because they may be more important.

Figure 6.6. Holistic Rubric for Work Done in a Graphic Organizer

Level of Performance	Description of the Level of Performance
Above Goal	The information meets all the criteria for "Goal" but it is especially well chosen. Examples and vocabulary make this work stand out.
Goal	The information is completely on the topic, accurate, of good quantity, and in the correct place in the graphic organizer. Most of the vocabulary is used accurately. The work is neat and presentable.
Needs Work	The information is mostly on the topic, mostly accurate, of reasonable quantity and mostly in the correct place in the graphic organizer. Vocabulary is not well chosen.

Figure 6.7. Holistic Rubric for
Work Done for the Student's Oral Presentation
of Work Done in a Graphic Organizer

Level of Performance	*Description of the Level of Performance*
Above Goal	The presentation meets all the criteria for work at "Goal." In addition, this presentation shows special insight into the task, and presents unusually interesting details. The student does an especially good job of using enthusiasm, voice, and body language to keep the attention of the audience.
Goal	The presentation is entirely on the topic. The information is presented according to the pattern of the graphic organizer, i.e., a sequence, a comparison with details, or a prediction with support. The vocabulary is adequate. The student uses a few details to show that he or she understands the topic. The student speaks in a reasonably good group-sharing voice.
Needs Work	The presentation is mostly on the topic. The information is mostly presented according to the pattern of the graphic organizer, i.e., a sequence, a comparison with details, or a prediction with support. Vocabulary is not well used and there are too few details to show that he understands the topic. The student's presentation voice is not of sufficient energy for all to hear.

Creating Ideas for Performance Tasks

The first step in creating performance tasks is to generate ideas for each of the four levels of comprehension. Figure 6.8 shows ideas generated for various versions of the "Cinderella" story. Figures 6.9 through Figure 6.16 (pages 118 through 125) show ideas generated for the study of the books: *Number the Stars; Fudge-a-mania; Ramona Quimby, Age 8; Junebug; Incredible Journey of Lewis & Clark; A Frontier Fort on the Oregon Trail;* a collection of books on the heart and circulation system; and a collection of books on the weather.

The ideas for these performance tasks use one of the thinking-skill verbs. Performance tasks can be created that include two or more thinking-skill verbs, but those tasks would be longer. For example, a task could begin with a sequencing activity and conclude with a predicting activity. These tasks would include two graphic organizers, two assessment lists, and a "stop-and-check" point between the two parts of the performance tasks. It is good to start with simple tasks and move to more complex performance tasks when the students are ready for them.

Once ideas are generated, they will be made into performance tasks with assessment lists.

Figure 6.8. Ideas for Performance Tasks
for the Cinderella Collection

Book	Level of Comprehension	Verb(s)	Graphic Organizer	Ideas for Performance Tasks
Use a variety of books from the Cinderella collection.	Initial Understanding	Sequence	GO1	Show the sequence of events that happen in a Cinderella story.
	Developing an Interpretation	Infer	GO5	What are the attributes of human nature of a Cinderella?
	Making Connections	Interpret, Describe, Pattern	GO1, GO14, GO15	Create a storyboard for your own version of the Cinderella story involving the experiences of a child in an elementary school.
	Critical Stance	Judge	GO20	Did the drawings in the Cinderella stories make the stories more interesting?

Figure 6.9. Ideas for Performance Tasks for the Book, *Number the Stars*

Book and Activity	Level of Comprehension	Verb	Graphic Organizer	Ideas for Performance Tasks
Number the Stars	Initial Understanding	Describe	GO2	Describe the dangerous mission that Anne Marie was asked to go on.
	Developing an Interpretation	Describe Cause and Effect	GO17	What caused the Jews to want to leave Copenhagen?
	Making Connections	Generalize	GO13	Why do people keep secrets?
	Critical Stance	Extend	GO1	What happened to Anne Marie after Ellen Rosen left on the boat? Continue the story.

Figure 6.10. Ideas for Performance Tasks for the Book, *Ramona Quimby, Age 8*

Book and Activity	Level of Comprehension	Verb	Graphic Organizer	Ideas for Performance Tasks
Ramona Quimby, Age 8	Initial Understanding	Sequence	GO3	What events best show the beginning, middle and ending of the story?
	Developing an Interpretation	Draw Conclusions	GO11	How did Ramona's family deal with tough times?
	Making Connections	Compare	GO9	How were Ramona and Peter, in the story *Fudge a mania*, the same?
	Critical Stance	Judge	GO19	Did you like this story?

Figure 6.11. Ideas for Performance Tasks for the Book, *Junebug*

Book and Activity	Level of Comprehension	Verb	Graphic Organizer	Ideas for Performance Tasks
Junebug	Initial Understanding	Draw	Drawing	What is Junebug's dream?
	Developing an Interpretation	Hypothesize	GO5	Why did Junebug want to skip his birthday?
	Making Connections	Describe Relationship	GO7	What wish have you had and who helped it come true for you?
	Critical Stance	Judge	GO14 GO20	Did the author do a good job of describing the neighborhood where Junebug lived?

Figure 6.12. Ideas for Performance Tasks for the Book, *Fudge-a-mania*

Book and Activity	Level of Comprehension	Verb	Graphic Organizer	Ideas for Performance Tasks
Fudge-a-mania	Initial Understanding	Identify	GO13	List the funny things that happen in this story.
	Developing an Interpretation	Interpret	GO16	Select one of the characters and interpret what that character thinks about him or herself.
	Making Connections	Compare and Contrast	GO8	Compare and contrast yourself to any one of the characters in Fudge-a-mania.
	Critical Stance	Evaluate	GO20	Evaluate the job Judy Blume did to make the characters believable.

Figure 6.13. Ideas for Performance Tasks for Books about the Great Explorers

Book and Activity	Level of Comprehension	Verb	Graphic Organizer	Ideas for Performance Tasks
The Incredible Journey of Lewis and Clark	Initial Understanding	List	GO13	What were the reasons for the Lewis and Clark expedition?
	Developing an Interpretation	Describe, Summarize	GO10	Gather information for a newspaper story on what the Lewis and Clark expedition accomplished?
	Making Connections	Compare and Contrast	GO8	Compare and contrast the expedition of Lewis and Clark to the expedition of Columbus.
	Critical Stance	Judge	GO20	Judge how the author, Rhoda Blumberg, portrayed the Native Americans.

Figure 6.14. Ideas for Performance Tasks for Books about the Westward Movement

Book and Activity	Level of Comprehension	Verb	Graphic Organizer	Ideas for Performance Tasks
A Frontier Fort on the Oregon Trail	Initial Understanding	Describe	GO12	Describe the experience of being inside the fort.
	Developing an Interpretation	Explain	GO5	How safe would you be in a fort?
	Making Connections	Compare	GO9	Compare the most important possessions of your own family to the most important possessions of a family traveling west on the Oregon Trail.
	Initial Understanding, Developing an Interpretation, Making Connections and Critical Stance	Sequence, Analyze, Judge	GO18, GO21	Find information to help answer this research question, "Why was a fort on the Oregon Trail important to the Westward Movement?"

Figure 6.15. Ideas for Performance Tasks
for Books about the Heart

Book and Activity	Level of Comprehension	Verb	Graphic Organizer	Ideas for Performance Tasks
• *The Magic School Bus Inside the Human Body* • *The Heart* • *Human Body* • *Transport Systems* • *others*	Initial Understanding	Describe	Drawing	Did I draw a realistic picture of the human heart?
	Developing an Interpretation and Making Connections	Analyze, Examine, Interpret, Summarize	GO18	How does the heart work?
	Critical Stance	Evaluate	GO21	Which of the books about the heart was the most helpful in your research? Why?

Figure 6.16. Ideas for Performance Tasks for Books about Hurricanes and Tornadoes

Book and Activity	Level of Comprehension	Verb	Graphic Organizer	Ideas for Performance Tasks
• *Tornadoes* • *Hurricanes* • *Weatherwise Learning about the Weather* • *Understanding the Atmosphere* • *others*	Initial Understanding, Developing an Interpretatio, Making Connections	Analyze, Compare, Contrast, Examine, Interpret, Summarize	GO7, GO11	Select one of the following questions and find information to help answer it. • How do hurricanes and tornadoes move? • What do a hurricane and a tornado look like? • When and where do hurricanes and tornadoes form? • What makes a hurricane and a tornado move? • What damage can a hurricane and a tornado do?
	Making Connections	Compare and Contrast	GO9, GO21	How are hurricanes and tornadoes the same and different?

Creating the Performance Tasks

The strategies for creating a performance task are presented in Chapter 5. Some highlights of that process are presented here:

- ◆ Write the performance task the student will have to perform. The task should be no more than one page long.
- ◆ **Background** provides a context for the task.
- ◆ **Task** states what the student will make and/or do.
- ◆ **Audience** describes who will be viewing or hearing the student's work. Try to find opportunities for the student work to really be viewed or heard by people outside of your classroom.
- ◆ **Purpose** describes how the student's work will impact the audience.
- ◆ The **Procedure** is a simple list of the steps to take in order. Let the assessment list provide the details. For example, a step in the procedure may state, "Use the vocabulary words from our unit." An item in the assessment list may state, "Did I use at least six of the vocabulary words from the unit?"

Creating Assessment Lists

The point of an assessment list is to help the students pay attention to as much about the quality of their work as possible. When students are doing work in graphic organizers, the assessment list must include items directly related to the type of thinking required by that assessment list. For example, if the student is doing work in a graphic organizer that asks for contrasts and comparisons, the items in the assessment list must reflect that requirement. Figure 6.38 presents an assessment list for the work done in graphic organizer GO8 which is a Venn Diagram. The thinking skill is to compare and contrast. Items four through six in that assessment list focus on comparing and contrasting. Those items are the most important part of that assessment list, so they have the most points. When the teacher makes the assessment list for student work in a graphic organizer, the teacher studies the graphic organizer and writes items for the assessment list that state what the student is required to do in that graphic organizer.

All the other strategies used to create assessment lists presented in the previous chapters are used here to create assessment lists that help students pay attention to the quality of their work. Assessment lists for the work done in drawings, graphic organizers that require written language, and oral presentations should be used in whole-class activities, small-group work, and individual work. A summary of some of the points to remember when creating assessment lists are presented here:

- Limit the number of items on the assessment list to the number of items the students will pay attention to.
- Word the items so that each is very specific.
- Attend to only one aspect of the work in any one item.
- Include "Sure Thing" items referring to aspects of the work that the students do well.
- Include one "Challenge" item to coach new learning.
- Ask the students to help create assessment lists when possible.

The Options for the Format of Assessment Lists

The following list presents several strategies for using assessment lists during whole-class, small-group, and individual work.

- **Large Classroom Posters**

  Assessment lists for commonly used graphic organizers can be created on poster board and used repeatedly during the year when that graphic organizer is used. Used in this way, the poster version of the assessment list is well-suited to whole-group work or for activities in centers.

- **Small Posters**

  Assessment lists can be created on small posters and placed in centers for activities using graphic organizers.

- **Assessment Lists On Paper**

  Assessment lists on regular paper can be used when it is desirable for the student to mark the paper to show self-assessment. The teacher then marks the assessment list to show their opinion of the student's work. The teacher may also write comments on the paper and use the assessment list during student conferences.

When the assessment lists are on paper they can be sent home, saved in the student's portfolio, posted in the room or hall bulletin board, and used during parent conferences.

Coaching the Students to Use Assessment Lists Accurately

Students use the assessment list to pay attention to their work before they start, while they are working, and when they have completed the performance task. They assign points to each item in the assessment list when their work is done. Often, students are accurate in self-assessment. But when they are inaccurate, the teacher must coach them to pay more attention to the details of the work that they assessed inaccurately.

If there are 15 points possible for "putting information in all parts of the graphic organizer," and the student has left some parts blank, the teacher asks the student to point out each part of the graphic organizer and state what information is included. When the student focuses on his work this closely, his self-assessment is usually more accurate. If the student is still inaccurate, the teacher shows the student models of student work that shows a graphic organizer completed correctly. The point is to gently coach the student to focus on the erroneous aspect of his work and compare it to work that is well done.

Asking Students to Help Create the Assessment List

After the students have had experience using an assessment list with a specific type of graphic organizer, they can help in creating assessment lists for that kind of graphic organizer when it is used again. This active involvement in creating the assessment list teaches them more about paying attention to the quality of their work and improving their performance. The goal is to coach students to become more independent in their learning.

Assigning Points to Items in Assessment Lists and Scoring Student Work

Figure 6.17 shows what Terrific, Okay, and Needs Work are worth.

Figure 6.17. Scores for the Three Levels of Performance

When the Most Points Possible Is:	Terrific Performance Is Worth:	Okay Performance Is Worth:	Needs Work Performance Is Worth:
3	3	2	1
6	6–5	4–3	2–0
9	9–7	6–4	3–0
12	12–9	8–5	4–0
15	15–11	10–6	5–0
18	18–13	12–7	6–0
21	21–15	14–8	7–0
24	24–17	16–9	8–0
27	27–19	18–10	9–0
30	30–21	20–11	10–0

Refer to the assessment list in Figure 6.22 that is used with the performance task entitled, *Attributes of Human Nature of a Cinderella*. Item three in that assessment list asks, "Did I find three pieces of good evidence from my reading and put them into my graphic organizer?" That item is worth, at most, 15 points. A score of Terrific on that item would earn the student 15 points (five points for each of the three pieces of good evidence.) If the student had only two pieces of good evidence, the student would get 10 points. One piece of good evidence would be worth five points. In the case of this item relating to three good pieces of evidence, it is clear how the student would earn 15 or 10 or 5 points.

The scoring of some items is not so straightforward. Figure 6.40 is the assessment list that accompanies the performance task entitled, *Extra! Extra! Read about Lewis and Clark*. Refer to element four in Figure 6.40, which reads, "I explained why." The most a student could earn on that element is 24 points. The table in Figure 6.17 shows that a "Terrific" performance is worth between 24 and 17 points, an Okay performance between 16 and 9 points, and a Needs Work performance between 8 and 0 points. The student, during self-assessment, and the teacher, during final assessment, must make a judgment about exactly how many points the student's actual performance is worth. If the actual performance is in the "Terrific" range, is it a "High Terrific" and worth 24 points, or is it a "Low Terrific, worth only 17 points? This kind of scoring is not always completely objective. The conversations that teachers and students have about what quality means helps everyone develop a clearer understanding of where a student's work fits on the continuum of points, and enhances the student's understanding and performance.

Prior to an assessment list like this one being used, the teacher and students must look at student work and talk about what makes a performance Terrific, Okay, or Needs Work. The conversation continues to address the idea of what makes Terrific work highly Terrific or only just barely Terrific. The ranges for Okay and Needs Work are also discussed. It is essential that these conversations occur for any item on an assessment list for which there may be some confusion about scoring.

Giving Students a Grade for a Report Card

Assessment is giving students feedback on the strengths and weaknesses of their performance, and an analytic rubric or an assessment list provides this detailed feedback. The information from assessment lists help students and teachers celebrate good work and focus on what needs attention next.

A grade is an overall rating of the student's performance. The overall rating could be done using a holistic rubric. For example, Figure 6.6 is a holistic rubric for doing work in a graphic organizer, and the student's work could be rated or graded "Above Goal," "At Goal," or "Near Goal." This rating or grade can be used to describe where a student is in relationship to his past performance, in relationship to a goal set for him, or in relationship to the performance of other students. The rating or grade does not provide information to the student or teacher about specific strengths or weaknesses of the student's work.

A student's work can be assessed and graded. Many school districts continue to use grades for report cards, and total scores from assessment lists can be easily converted into grades, as demonstrated in Figure 6.18.

Figure 6.18. Converting Assessment Points into Grades

Percentage of the total points	*Grade for the report cards*
90%	A
80%	B
70%	C
60%	D
Below 60%	F

Figure 6.26 presents an assessment list with 68 total possible points. Ninety percent of 68 is 61 points, so a score of 61 or higher would be an "A." Eighty percent of 68 is 54, so a score of 54 to 60 would be a "B." Seventy percent of 68 is 47, so a score of 47 to 53 would be a "C," a score of 41 to 46 would be a "D," and a score of 40 or below would be a "F." Plusses and minuses could also be given.

A score of 60 would be a "B+," a score of 57 would be a "B," and a score of 54 would be a "B-."

Figure 6.19. Performance Task:
Storyboard for Cinderella

Background

You have read many versions of the Cinderella story. They all have a common theme and a sequence of events.

Task

Your task is to create a storyboard for the common sequence of events that happen in these different Cinderella stories.

Audience

The library/media teacher will use your storyboards to advertise the "Cinderella" books in the school library.

Purpose

The purpose of your storyboard is to interest other students in reading some of Cinderella stories.

Procedure

1. Review the assessment list for this task.
2. Get graphic organizer GO1.
3. Put the information into the graphic organizer.
4. Use your assessment list to self-assess.
5. Turn your graphic organizer and assessment list into your teacher.

Figure 6.20. Performance Task Assessment List: Storyboard for Cinderella

Graphic Organizer GO1

	Item	Assessment Points Possible	Points Earned	
			Assessed by Self	Assessed by Teacher
1.	Did I put my name and date at the top of the graphic organizer page?	3	_____	_____
2.	Did I use GO1?	3	_____	_____
3.	Did I show the beginning parts of the story?	6	_____	_____
4.	Did I show the middle parts of the story?	6	_____	_____
5.	Did I show the ending parts of the story?	6	_____	_____
6.	Did I use enough details to show what was happening?	6	_____	_____
7.	Is my work neat?	3	_____	_____
8.	Did I finish my work on time?	3	_____	_____
	Total	**36**	_____	_____

Figure 6.21. Performance Task:
Attributes of Human Nature of a Cinderella

Background

You have read the "Cinderella" stories, which are set in many different cultures around the world. What are the common attributes of human nature of a "Cinderella?"

Task

Select one important attribute of human nature of a "Cinderella" and show the evidence for your decision in a graphic organizer.

Audience

Good citizenship and character education is important in your school. These programs are important to your principal. You will give your graphic organizers to your principal.

Purpose

The purpose of your graphic organizer is to inform the principal about the attributes of human nature of a "Cinderella."

Procedure

1. Review the assessment list for this task.
2. Get graphic organizer GO5.
3. Put the information into the graphic organizer.
4. Use your assessment list to self-assess.
5. Turn your graphic organizer and assessment list into your teacher.

Figure 6.22. Performance Task Assessment List: Attributes of Human Nature of a Cinderella

Graphic Organizer GO5

Item	Assessment Points Possible	Points Earned	
		Assessed by Self	Assessed by Teacher
1. Did I put my name and date at the top of the graphic organizer page?	3	_____	_____
2. Did I select one attribute of human nature that is important for a Cinderella?	9	_____	_____
3. Did I find three pieces of good evidence from my reading and put them into the graphic organizer?	15	_____	_____
4. Did I indicate the page number reference for each piece of evidence?	9	_____	_____
5. Did I use complete sentences?	6	_____	_____
6. Does my work look organized?	3	_____	_____
Total	**45**	_____	_____

Figure 6.23. Performance Task:
A Cinderella Story in an Elementary School

Background

You have read Cinderella stories from all over the world, but you have not read any Cinderella stories that took place in an elementary school. Your job is to create a storyboard and other information that you could use to write your own Cinderella story about a child in an elementary school.

The behavior of a Cinderella or Cinderfella, and the people in their life, teach us important lessons about respecting each other.

Task

The task is to create the graphic organizers for a story. (You will not write the story now.) The procedure will tell you which graphic organizers to use.

Be sure to make your character fictional so that no student in your school thinks the story is about them.

Audience

The guidance counselor in your school wants to use your story ideas for help in teaching what being respectful to others means.

Purpose

The purpose of your story ideas is to entertain and to teach the guidance counselor and other students what being respectful to others means.

Proceure

1. Review the assessment list for this task.
2. Use the following graphic organizers and do them in this order:
   - GO1 for the storyboard (page 168)
   - GO14 for the setting (page 184)
   - GO15 for the Cinderella or Cinderfella character of your story (page 185)
   - GO1 revise your storyboard (page 168)
3. Do one graphic organizer at a time, and get approval from your teacher before you start the next graphic organizer.
4. Put the information into the graphic organizers.
5. Use your assessment list to self-assess.
6. Turn your graphic organizers and assessment lists into your teacher.

Figure 6.24. Performance Task Assessment List: A Cinderella Story in an Elementary School

Graphic Organizer GO1

	Item	Assessment Points Possible	Points Earned	
			Assessed by Self	Assessed by Teacher
1.	Did I use GO1?	3	_____	_____
2.	Did I show the beginning parts of the story?	6	_____	_____
3.	Did I show the middle parts of the story?	6	_____	_____
4.	Did I show the ending parts of the story?	6	_____	_____
5.	Did I use enough details to show what was happening?	6	_____	_____
6.	Is my work neat?	3	_____	_____
7.	Did I finish my work on time?	3	_____	_____
	Total	**33**	_____	_____

Figure 6.25. Performance Task Assessment List:
A Cinderella Story in an Elementary School

Graphic Organizer GO18

| | | Points Earned | |
Item	Assessment Points Possible	Assessed by Self	Assessed by Teacher
1. Did I draw a picture of the setting?	15	_____	_____
2. Did I use color for emphasis?	6	_____	_____
3. Did I show details?	6	_____	_____
4. Did I show background, middleground, and foreground?	9	_____	_____
5. Did I write descriptive words for all four senses?	15	_____	_____
6. Did I spell the descriptive words correctly?	6	_____	_____
7. Is my work neat?	6	_____	_____
Total	63	_____	_____

Figure 6.26. Performance Task Assessment List: A Cinderella Story in an Elementary School

Graphic Organizer GO19

| | | | Points Earned | |
	Item	Assessment Points Possible	Assessed by Self	Assessed by Teacher
1.	Did I draw a picture of my Cinderella or Cinderfella character?	6	_____	_____
2.	Did I show details of the face?	9	_____	_____
3.	Did I show details of the clothing?	9	_____	_____
4.	Did show details of any unusual characteristics so my character would be interesting?	12	_____	_____
5.	Did I use color for emphasis?	6	_____	_____
6.	Did I list descriptive words for size, features, clothing, facial expression, and any unusual characteristics?	15	_____	_____
7.	Did I spell my words correctly?	6	_____	_____
8.	Did I finish my work on time?	6	_____	_____
	Total	68	_____	_____

Figure 6.27. Performance Task Assessment List: A Cinderella Story in an Elementary School

Graphic Organizer GO1

| | | | Points Earned | |
	Item	Assessment Points Possible	Assessed by Self	Assessed by Teacher
1.	Did I revise the beginning parts of the story?	6	_____	_____
2.	Did I revise the middle parts of the story?	6	_____	_____
3.	Did I revise the ending parts of the story?	6	_____	_____
4.	Did I use enough details to show what was happening?	6	_____	_____
5.	Did I use details from the setting I created?	6	_____	_____
6.	Did I use details from the character I created?	6	_____	_____
7.	Overall, does my story follow the Cinderella pattern?	30	_____	_____
8.	Is my work neat?	3	_____	_____
9.	Did I finish my work on time?	3	_____	_____
	Total	72	_____	_____

Figure 6.28. Performance Task:
The Power of Illustrations

Background

It is interesting to read the different versions of Cinderella. How important do you think drawings are to keep the reader interested in the stories?

Task

Your task is to judge the work of the illustrators and select the illustrator you think did the best job of using drawings to make the story interesting.

Audience

Your art teacher wants to display the work of good illustrators along with your critique of their work. The display will be put in the display area in the hall near the principal's office.

Purpose

The purpose of the display with your critique is to teach the visitors to the school about the importance of illustrations in telling a story.

Procedure

1. Review the assessment list for this task.
2. Get graphic organizer GO20.
3. Put the information into the graphic organizer.
4. Use your assessment list to self-assess.
5. Turn your graphic organizer and assessment list into your teacher.

Figure 6.29. Performance Task Assessment List: The Power of Illustrations

Graphic Organizer GO20

| | | | Points Earned | |
	Item	Assessment Points Possible	Assessed by Self	Assessed by Teacher
1.	Did I select an illustrator and put their name and title of the book on the line above the arrows?	9	_____	_____
2.	Did I select Yes or No to show if I thought this illustrator did a good job of using illustrations to make the story more interesting?	9	_____	_____
3.	Did I list at least three reasons for my opinion?	15	_____	_____
4.	Did I use the information in the text, including the illustrations, to support my opinion?	15	_____	_____
5.	Did I use complete sentences?	6	_____	_____
6.	Did I start each sentence with a capital and end it with a punctuation mark?	6	_____	_____
7.	Is my work neat?	6	_____	_____
	Total	**66**	_____	_____

Figure 6.30. Performance Task: Why Did the Jews Leave Copenhagen?

Background
Ellen Rosen and the other Jews living in Copenhagen desperately needed to get out of Denmark. Why? The class is doing research on what happened to the Jews and other people during World War II.

Task
Find information in the story and use your own knowledge to make research notes.

Audience
These research notes are for your notebook.

Purpose
You will use them to help you with other assignments later in this unit.

Procedure
1. Review the assessment list for this task.
2. Get graphic organizer GO17.
3. Put the information into the graphic organizer.
4. Use your assessment list to self-assess.
5. Turn your graphic organizer and assessment list into your teacher.

Figure 6.31. Performance Task Assessment List: Why Did the Jews Leave Copenhagen?

Graphic Organizer GO17

	Item	Assessment Points Possible	Points Earned Assessed by Self	Points Earned Assessed by Teacher
1.	Did I copy the research question from the board into the top box on my paper?	3	_____	_____
2.	Did I find at least three pieces of information in the story to help me answer the research question?	18	_____	_____
3.	Did I write my thoughts next to each of the pieces of information?	18	_____	_____
4.	Did I use complete sentences?	6	_____	_____
5.	Is my work neat?	6	_____	_____
	Total	**51**	_____	_____

Figure 6.32. Performance Task:
Sequence of Events in *Ramona Quimby, Age 8*

Background

A lot of things happened to Ramona Quimby. What are the most important events in this story?

Task

Your task is to describe one important event at the beginning, one important event in the middle, and one important event at the end of the story.

Audience

Your graphic organizers will be put on our bulletin board for open house night for parents to see.

Purpose

Your work will show your parents that you are learning about how stories are written.

Procedure

1. Review the assessment list for this task.
2. Get graphic organizer GO3.
3. Put the information into the graphic organizer.
4. Draw a simple sketch and write a description for each event.
5. Use your assessment list to self-assess.
6. Turn your graphic organizer and assessment list into your teacher.

Figure 6.33. Performance Task Assessment List: Sequence of Events in *Ramona Quimby, Age 8*

Graphic Organizer GO3

	Item	Assessment Points Possible	Points Earned Assessed by Self	Points Earned Assessed by Teacher
1.	Did I draw a simple sketch for each event?	9	_____	_____
2.	Did I write a description of each event?	9	_____	_____
3.	Did I describe one important event at the beginning of the story?	6	_____	_____
4.	Did I describe one important event in the middle of the story?	6	_____	_____
5.	Did I describe one important event at the end of the story?	6	_____	_____
6.	Did I spell my words correctly?	3	_____	_____
7.	Is my work neat?	3	_____	_____
	Total	**42**	_____	_____

Figure 6.34. Performance Task:
Junebug's Neighborhood

Background

We are leaning about the neighborhoods people live in all around the world. For Social Studies and Art, we are drawing pictures to show what these neighborhoods look like.

Task

Your task is to draw a picture of Junebug's neighborhood based on Alice Mead's description.

Audience

All of our drawings of the neighborhoods will be displayed in the town hall for the people who go there to do business.

Purpose

The purpose of your drawing is to teach people about all the different kinds of neighborhoods where people live.

Procedure

1. Review the assessment list for this task.
2. Use graphic organizer GO14 to draw a picture of Junebug's neighborhood.
3. Use graphic organizer GO20 to judge the quality of the descriptions Alice Mead makes of Junebug's neighborhood.
4. Use your assessment list to self-assess.
5. Turn your two graphic organizers and assessment list into your teacher.

Figure 6.35. Performance Task Assessment List: Junebug's Neighborhood

Graphic Organizer GO14

	Item	Assessment Points Possible	Points Earned Assessed by Self	Assessed by Teacher
1.	Did I draw a picture of Junebug's neighborhood?	12	_____	_____
2.	Did I draw details?	12	_____	_____
3.	Did I show background, middleground, and foreground?	6	_____	_____
4.	Did I use color for emphasis?	6	_____	_____
5.	Did I use texture for emphasis?	6	_____	_____
6.	Did I include descriptive words for each of the four senses?	12	_____	_____
7.	Did I write the page numbers from the book on my drawing to show where I got information to draw this picture?	24	_____	_____
8.	Is my work neat and was it completed on time?	6	_____	_____
	Total	**84**	_____	_____

Figure 6.36. Performance Task Assessment List: Junebug's Neighborhood

Graphic Organizer GO20

Item	Assessment Points Possible	Points Earned Assessed by Self	Assessed by Teacher
1. Did I decide whether or not Alice Mead did a good job of describing Junebug's neighborhood?	24	_____	_____
2. Did I give at least four reasons for my position?	24	_____	_____
3. Did I list the page number to show where I got my evidence?	24	_____	_____
Total	72	_____	_____

Figure 6.37. Performance Task:
Who Are You Most Like in *Fudge-a-mania*?

Background

Judy Blume is famous for writing stories that have very realistic characters. Which one of those characters is most like you?

Task

You job is to select the character that is most like you and to complete a Venn Diagram for you and that character.

Audience

You will take your Venn Diagram home to your parents.

Purpose

The purpose of your Venn Diagram is to entertain your parents.

Procedure

1. Review the assessment list for this task.
2. Get graphic organizer GO8.
3. Put the information into the graphic organizer.
4. Use your assessment list to self-assess.
5. Turn your graphic organizer and assessment list into your teacher.

Figure 6.38. Performance Task Assessment List: Who Are You Most Like in *Fudge-a-mania*?

Graphic Organizer GO8

Items	Assessment Points Possible	Points Earned	
		Assessed by Self	Assessed by Teacher
1. Did I put my name and date on my paper.	3	_____	_____
2. Did I write my name by "A?"	3	_____	_____
3. Did I select one character and write their name by "B?"	3	_____	_____
4. Did I list at least three special things about me that are not true about that character?	12	_____	_____
5. Did I list at least three special things about the character that are not true about me?	12	_____	_____
6. Did I list three ways the character and I are the same?	15	_____	_____
7. Is my spelling correct?	6	_____	_____
8. Is my work is neat?	3	_____	_____
9. Did I finish my work on time?	3	_____	_____
Total	57	_____	_____

Figure 6.39. Performance Task:
Extra! Extra! Read About Lewis and Clark

Background

The Lewis and Clark expedition was an exciting adventure. People would be interested in hearing news about the expedition.

Task

Pretend that you are a news reporter traveling with Lewis and Clark. Your task is to make notes for a newspaper article that you might write when you get back home.

Audience

Your teacher is pretending to be the editor of the newspaper. Your teacher will read your notes.

Purpose

If your notes impress the "editor," she will let you write an article for the newspaper.

Procedure

1. Review the assessment list for this task.
2. Get graphic organizer GO10.
3. Put the information into the graphic organizer.
4. Use your assessment list to self-assess.
5. Turn your graphic organizer and assessment list into your teacher.

Figure 6.40. Performance Task Assessment List: Extra! Extra! Read About Lewis and Clark

Graphic Organizer 10

		Item	Assessment Points Possible	Points Earned	
				Assessed by Self	Assessed by Teacher
1.		Did I select an exciting part of the expedition on which to report?	15	_____	_____
2.		Did I report on the Who, What, and When?	15	_____	_____
3.		Did I explain How?	15	_____	_____
4.		Did I explain Why?	24	_____	_____
5.		Did I use complete sentences?	9	_____	_____
6.		Did I spell my words correctly?	6	_____	_____
7.		Is my work neat?	3	_____	_____
		Total	87	_____	_____

Figure 6.41. Performance Task:
What Is It Like to Be Inside a Fort on the Oregon Trail?

Background

Pretend that you are a Native American, a solider, or a member of a wagon train. What is it like inside a fort on the Oregon Trail?

Task

Your task is to record your impressions of what it is like to be inside a fort on the Oregon Trail.

Audience

Your family back home will be the audience for your thoughts.

Purpose

The purpose of your notes is to help your family get a better feeling about what it is like inside a fort on the Oregon Trail.

Procedure

1. Review the assessment list for this task.
2. Get graphic organizer GO12.
3. Put the information into the graphic organizer.
4. Use your assessment list to self-assess.
5. Turn your graphic organizer and assessment list into your teacher.

Figure 6.42. Performance Task Assessment List: What Is It Like to Be Inside a Fort on the Oregon Trail?

Graphic Organizer GO12

	Item	Assessment Points Possible	Points Earned	
			Assessed by Self	Assessed by Teacher
1.	Did I write my topic in the center oval?	6	_____	_____
2.	Did I list at least three pieces of information for "I see?"	9	_____	_____
3.	Did I list at least three pieces of information for "I hear?"	9	_____	_____
4.	Did I list at least three pieces of information for "I smell?"	9	_____	_____
5.	Did I list at least three pieces of information for "I feel?"	9	_____	_____
6.	Did I spell my words correctly?	6	_____	_____
7.	Is my work neat?	6	_____	_____
	Total	**54**	_____	_____

Figure 6.43. Performance Task: You Can't Beat the Heart

Background

The heart is one of the parts of our bodies that we need to live. How much do you know about how the heart works?

Task

You will do some research and take notes about how the heart works.

Audience

When you finish your notes, you will plan a presentation that you will make to some first-grade students who are learning about the human body.

Purpose

The purpose of your notes is to help you prepare to teach the first graders.

Procedure

1. Review the assessment list for this task.
2. Get graphic organizer GO18.
3. Put the information into the graphic organizer.
4. Use your assessment list to self-assess.
5. Turn your graphic organizer and assessment list into your teacher.

Figure 6.44. Performance Task Assessment List:
You Can't Beat the Heart

Graphic Organizer GO18

	Item	Assessment Points Possible	Points Earned	
			Assessed by Self	Assessed by Teacher
1.	Did I put my name and today's date at the top of the page?	3	_____	_____
2.	Did I write my research question at the top of the graphic organizer?	3	_____	_____
3.	Did I list what I already know about the heart?	12	_____	_____
4.	Did I list questions I have about the heart and how it works?	12	_____	_____
5.	Did I list information that would help me answer my questions?	12	_____	_____
6.	If I needed more space, did I use additional sheets of paper to continue my notes?	6	_____	_____
7.	Did I use complete sentences?	6	_____	_____
8.	Did I use correct end punctuation?	6	_____	_____
9.	Is my work neat?	6	_____	_____
	Total	**66**	_____	_____

Figure 6.45. Performance Task: The Big Wind

Background

Hurricanes and tornadoes are huge, dangerous storms. How are they the same, and how are they different?

Task

Pretend that you are a weather person on the TV news. Your job is to get ready to explain how hurricanes and tornadoes are the same and different.

Audience

Your audience will be the people who watch that TV news program.

Purpose

The purpose of your notes is to help you get ready to teach the viewers how hurricanes and tornadoes are the same and how they are different.

Procedure

1. Review the assessment list for this task.
2. Get graphic organizers GO20 and GO8. You will need two copies of GO20.
3. Put the information into the graphic organizer.
4. Use your assessment list to self-assess.
5. Turn your graphic organizers and assessment list into your teacher.

Figure 6.46. Performance Task Assessment List: The Big Wind

Graphic Organizer GO20

Item	Assessment Points Possible	Points Earned	
		Assessed by Self	Assessed by Teacher
1. Did I use one paper for my research about hurricanes and a second paper for my research about tornadoes?	6	_____	_____
2. Did I put my name and the date at the top of each of my papers?	6	_____	_____
3. Did I write my research question in the top box?	6	_____	_____
4. Did I list at least six pieces of information about hurricanes?	24	_____	_____
5. Did I list at least six pieces of information about tornadoes?	24	_____	_____
6. Did I list the references for all of my information?	24	_____	_____
7. Did I write my thoughts about the notes for hurricanes?	36	_____	_____
8. Did I write my thoughts about the notes for tornadoes?	36	_____	_____
9. Did I use complete sentences?	6	_____	_____
10. Is my work neat?	6	_____	_____
Total	**174**	_____	_____

Figure 6.47. Performance Task Assessment List: The Big Wind

Graphic Organizer GO8

	Item	Assessment Points Possible	Points Earned	
			Assessed by Self	Assessed by Teacher
1.	Did I write my name and date at the top of the paper?	6	_____	_____
2.	Did I put the words hurricane and tornado in spaces "A" and "B?"	6	_____	_____
3.	Did I list at least three things that are true about hurricanes that are not true about tornadoes?	12	_____	_____
4.	Did I list at least three things that are true about tornadoes that are not true about hurricanes?	12	_____	_____
5.	Did I list at least five things that are the same for hurricanes and tornadoes?	15	_____	_____
6.	Did I spell my words correctly?	6	_____	_____
7.	Is my work neat?	6	_____	_____
	Total	63	_____	_____

Figure 6.48. Notes Regarding the Performance Tasks and Assessment Lists in This Chapter

Performance Task Title	Task	Assessment List	Comments
Storyboard for Cinderella	6.19		This is the first of four tasks using the Cinderella books for character ducation.
		6.20	Assessment list items are written to be questions the student asks himself.
Attributes of Human Nature of a Cinderella	6.21		The audience for the student's work is the principal. Many of the tasks in this chapter identify audiences other than the classroom teacher and fellow students.
		6.22	Items 1, 4, 5, and 6 are about processes and items 2 and 3 are focused on how well the stud ent understands the attributes of human nature exhibited by the Cinderella in the story.
A Cinderella Story in an Elementary School	6.23		This is a four-step task. The student creates a story-board, thinks more deeply about the character and setting, and then revises the story board.
		6.24	Each item is very specific.
		6.25	Elements and principles of art described in Chapter 4 are used here.
		6.26	This task will provide good opportunities to talk about how the student "defined" the character through the drawing.
		6.27	Students will enjoy sharing their stories.
The Power of Illustrations	6.28		This is a Critical Stance task.
		6.29	Items 5 and 6 address English mechanics.

Performance Task Title	Task	Assessment List	Comments
Why Did the Jews Leave Copenhagen?	6.30		This literature selection is used in an interdisciplinary unit with social studies.
		6.31	Item 2 is a "Sure Thing" because the student will do it well. Item 3 is a "Challenge" because students are not good at connecting their thoughts to research notes. The teacher will need to spend time modeling how to connect thoughts to research notes before the task is used.
Sequence of Events in *Ramona Quimby, Age 8*	6.32		When students are good at using graphic organizers about sequencing, ask them to make up their own graphic organizers for this kind of work.
		6.33	Each item addresses one specific part of the work. When students are more experienced, two or more parts can be combined in one item in the assessment list.
Junebug's Neighborhood	6.34		Here the student uses information in the story to draw a picture of Junebug's neighborhood. Then the student takes a Critical Stance as to how good the author's descriptions were to help the reader "visualize" what the neighborhood was like.
		6.35	Principles and elements of art are important in this task.
		6.36	This is a short, simple assessment list. Making one assessment list for both graphic organizers would have made the assessment list too long.
Who Are You Most Like in *Fudge-a-ma-nia*?	6.37		The parents are the audience for the student's work.
		6.38	The points for item 6 shows that it is the most important.
Extra! Extra! Read About Lewis & Clark	6.39		The student takes the role of newspaper reporter.
		6.40	The items in the assessment list follow the format of the graphic organizer.

Performance Task Title	Task	Assessment List	Comments
What Is It Like to Be Inside the Fort?	6.41		This task asks the student to generate sensory words to describe what it is like to be inside the fort.
		6.42	Each item in the assessment list is very specific.
You Can't Beat the Heart	6.43		Here the student is collecting information to make a presentation to first-grade students.
		6.44	Items three through six about taking notes are the most important and receives the most points.
The Big Wind	6.45		The student takes the role of TV weather person.
		6.46	Research notes can be taken from several sources.
		6.47	The student judges the quality of the information sources and identifies the ones that were the most helpful.

References

Variations on Cinderella (Used with Character Education)

Boada, F. (1997). *Cinderella/Cenicienta* (M. Fransoy, Illus.). San Francisco: Chronicle Books.

Brown, M. (1954). *Cinderella*. New York: Aladdin Paperbacks.

Climo, S. (1989). The *Egyptian Cinderella* (R. Heller, Illus.). New York: HarperCollins.

Climo, S. (1993). The *Korean Cinderella* (R. Heller, Illus.). New York: HarperCollins.

Climo, S. (1996). The *Irish Cindelad* (L. Krupinski, Illus.). New York: HarperCollins.

Hickox, R. (1998). The *Golden sandal* (W. Hillenbrand, Illus.). New York: Holiday House.

Huck, C. (1989). *Princess Furball* (A. Lobel, Illus.). New York: HarperCollins.

Jackson, E. (1994). *Cinder Edna* (K. O'Malley, Illus.). New York: Mulberry.

Karlin, B. (1989). *Cinderella* (J. Marshall, Illus.). Boston: Little, Brown.

Kinght, H. (1978). *Cinderella*. New York: Random House.

Louie, A. (1982). *Yeh-Shen a Cinderella Story From China* (E. Young, Illus.). New York: Philomel.

Martin, R. (1992). *The Rough-face Girl* (D. Shannon, Illus.). New York: Putnam.

Perrault, C. (1972). *Cinderella* (E. L. Cain, Trans. and Illus.). New York: Bradbury Press.

Perault, C. (1985). *Cinderella* (retold by A. Ehrlich; S. Jeffers, Illus.). New York: Dial Books.

Pollock, P. (1996). *The Turkey Girl* (E. Young, Illus.). Boston: Little, Brown.

San Souci, R. D.(1998). *Cendrillon* (B. Pinkney Illus.). New York: Simon & Schuster.

San Souci, R. D. (2000). *Little Gold Star* (S. Martinez, Illus.). New York: HarperCollins.

Schreder, A. (1997). *Smoky Mountain Rose* (B. Sneed, Illus.). New York: Penguin Books.

Literature Selections

Blume, J. (1983). *Fudge-a-mania*. New York: Bantam.

Cleary, B. (1981). *Ramona Quimby, age 8* (A. Tiegreen, Illus.). New York: Dell.

Lowry, L. (1989). *Number the Stars*. New York: Dell.

Mead, A. (1995). *Junebug*. Toronto: HarperCollins.

Exploration and the Westward Movement in American History

Blumberg, R. (1987). *The Incredible Journey of Lewis and Clark*. New York: Lothrop, Lee & Shepard Books.

Steedman, S. (1994). *A Frontier Fort on the Oregon Trail* (M. Bergin, Illus.). New York: Peter Bedrick Books.

The Heart

Cole, J. C. (1989). *The Magic School Bus Inside the Human Body* (B. Degen, Illus.). New York: Scholastic.

Parker, S. (1993). *Human Body Eyewitness Book*. New York: Dorling Kindersley.

Simon, S. (1996). *The Heart*. New York: Morrow Junior Books.

Staten Island Children's Museum. (1995). *Transport Systems: How Your Body Changes and Uses Food, Water and Air*. New York: Scholastic.

Weather

Kahl, J. D. (1992). *Weatherwise Learning About the Weather*. Minneapolis, MN.: Lerner.

Simon, S. (1999). *Tornaodes*. New York: Morrow Junior Books.

Souza, D. M. (1996). *Hurricanes*. Minneapolis, MN: Carolrhoda Books.

Appendix A

A Collection of Graphic Organizers

Graphic organizers GO1, GO5, GO8, GO15, and GO18 are accompanied by assessment lists. Sometimes "generic" assessment lists can be used in lieu of an assessment list tailored for specific applications of a graphic organizer.

Name _____   **Date:** _____

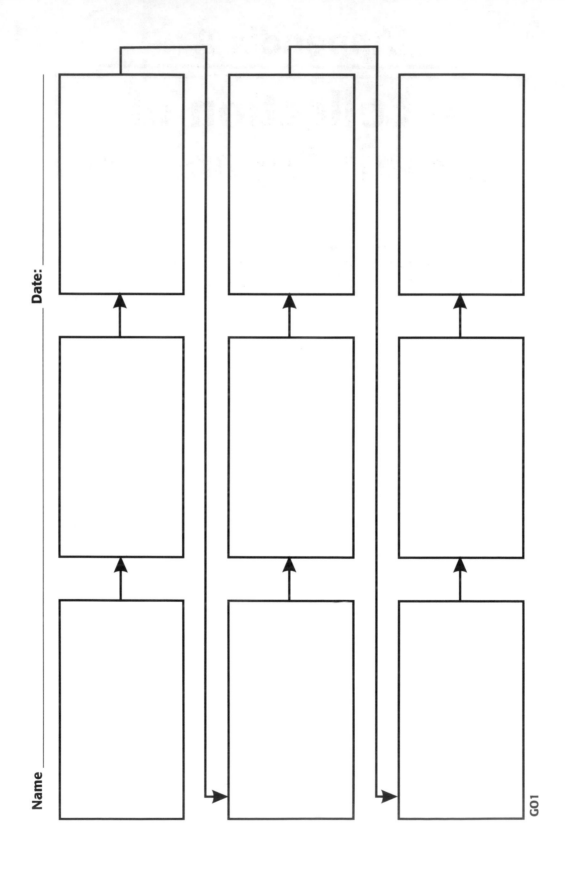

GO1

Performance Task Assessment List for
Graphic Organizer GO1: Sequencing

Item	Assessment Points Possible	Points Earned Assessed by Self	Assessed by Teacher
1. Did I put all the events in order from first to last?	_____	_____	_____
2. Is each item on my list accurate?	_____	_____	_____
3. Are all of the items I have selected the most important for this sequence?	_____	_____	_____
4. Is my spelling correct?	_____	_____	_____
5. Is my work neat and presentable?	_____	_____	_____
Total	_____	_____	_____

Name: _____ Date: _____

First, Then, Next, Last

First

Then

Next

Last

GO2

Name: _____ **Date:** _____

Book Title: _____

Beginning, Middle, and Ending

Beginning

Middle

Ending

GO3

Name: _____ **Date:** _____

Topic: _____

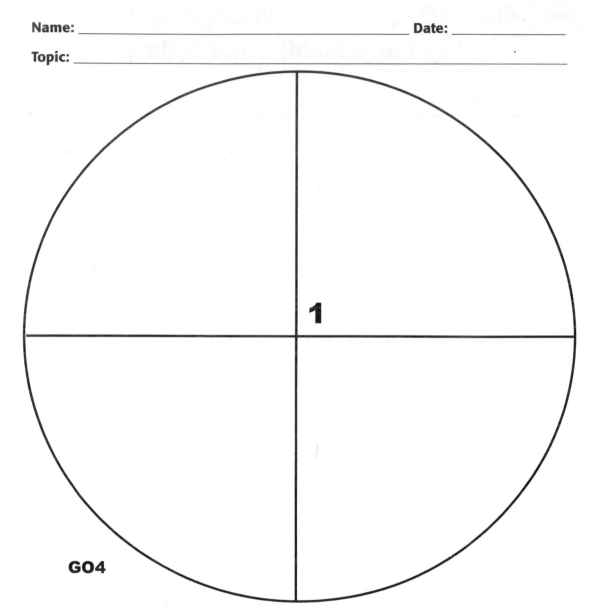

GO4

Divide the circle into as many pie-shaped wedges as necessary so that all of the steps in the cycle can be represented. Begin in space #1 and move clockwise. Number each space.

Performance Task Assessment List for Graphic Organizer GO5: Main Idea and Supporting Details

Item	Assessment Points Possible	Points Earned	
		Assessed by Self	Assessed by Teacher
1. Is my main idea accurate?	_____	_____	_____
2. Did I find three supporting details for my main idea?	_____	_____	_____
3. Is each detail accurate?	_____	_____	_____
4. Is each detail important support for my main idea?	_____	_____	_____
5. Did I use complete sentences?	_____	_____	_____
6. Did I use capitals and end punctuation correctly?	_____	_____	_____
7. Is my spelling correct?	_____	_____	_____
8. Is my work neat and presentable?	_____	_____	_____
Total	_____	_____	_____

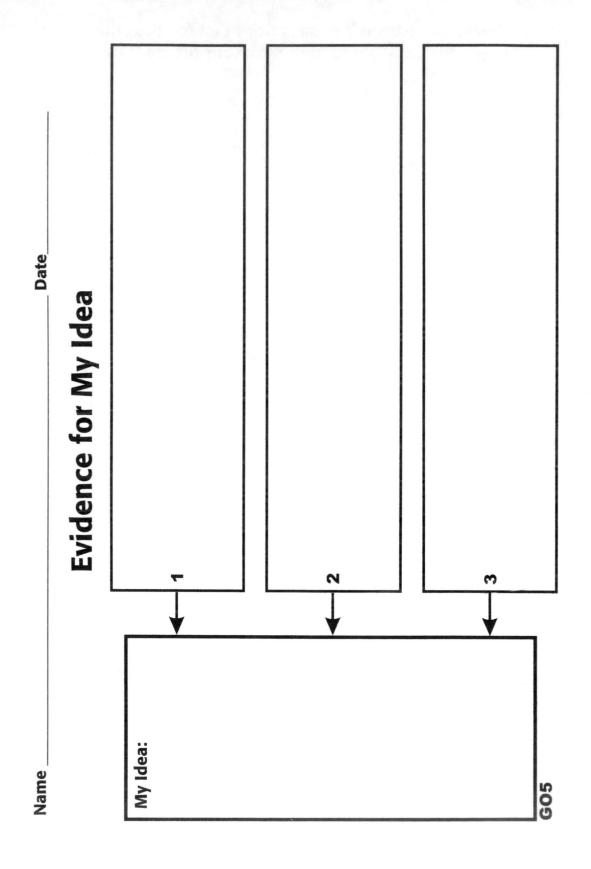

Name

Date

Evidence for My Idea

| 1 | 2 | 3 |

My Idea:

GO5

Name _____   Date _____

Make A Prediction

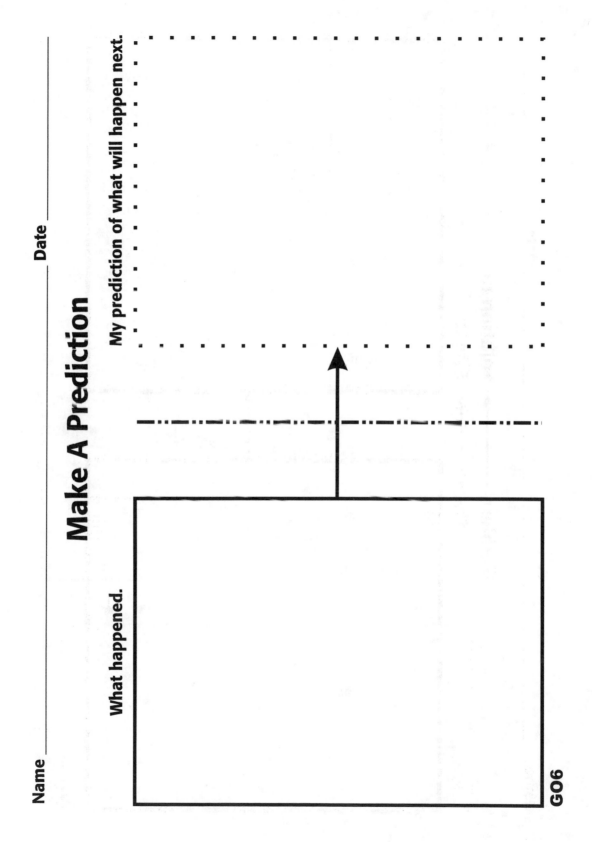

My prediction of what will happen next.

What happened.

GO6

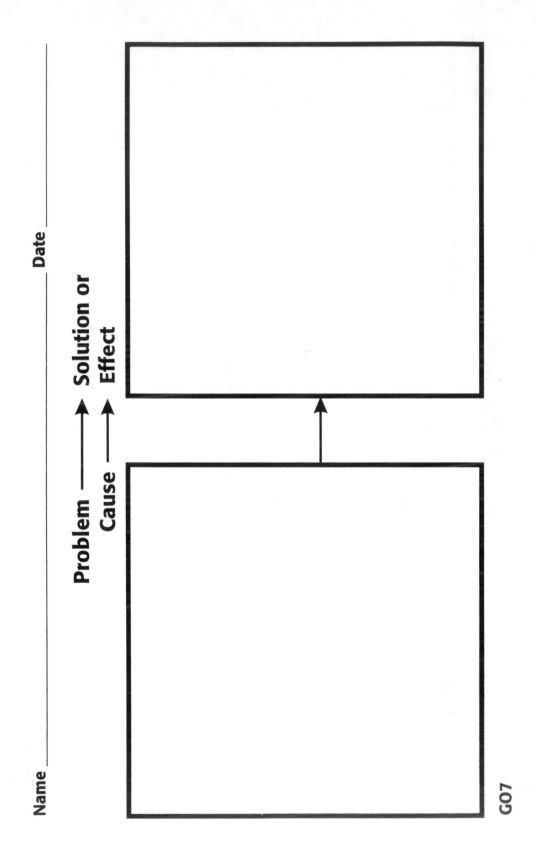

Name

Date

**Problem ➝ Solution or
Cause ➝ Effect**

G07

Name _____

Date _____

A and B
The Same

A _____

B _____

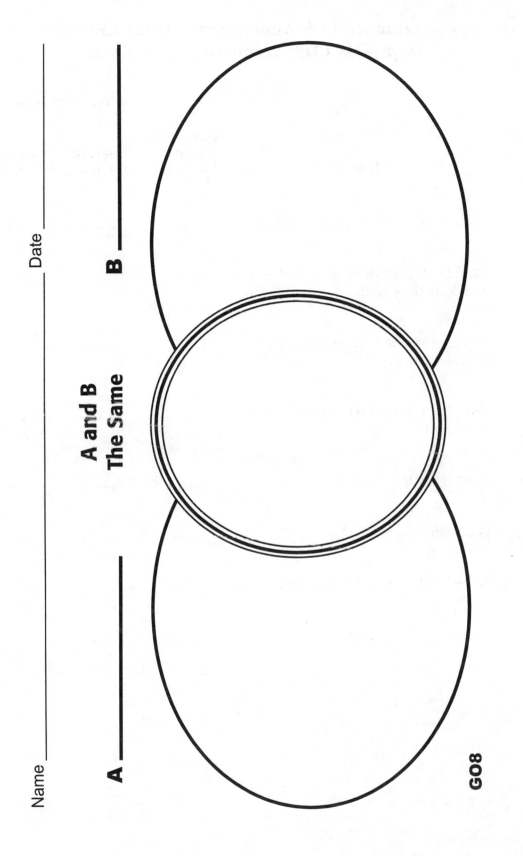

GO8

Performance Task Assessment List for Graphic Organizer GO8: Compare and Contrast

	Item	Assessment Points Possible	Points Earned Assessed by Self	Assessed by Teacher
1.	Did I write a title for A and for B?	_____	_____	_____
2.	Did I list at least three ways that A and B are the same?	_____	_____	_____
3.	Did I list at least three ways that A is different from B?	_____	_____	_____
4.	Did I list at least three ways that B is different from A?	_____	_____	_____
5.	Is all of my information correct?	_____	_____	_____
6.	Is my spelling correct?	_____	_____	_____
7.	Is my work neat and presentable?	_____	_____	_____
	Total	_____	_____	_____

Venn Diagram

Name _____   Date _____

Drawings and Words to Show Similarities or Differences (circle one)

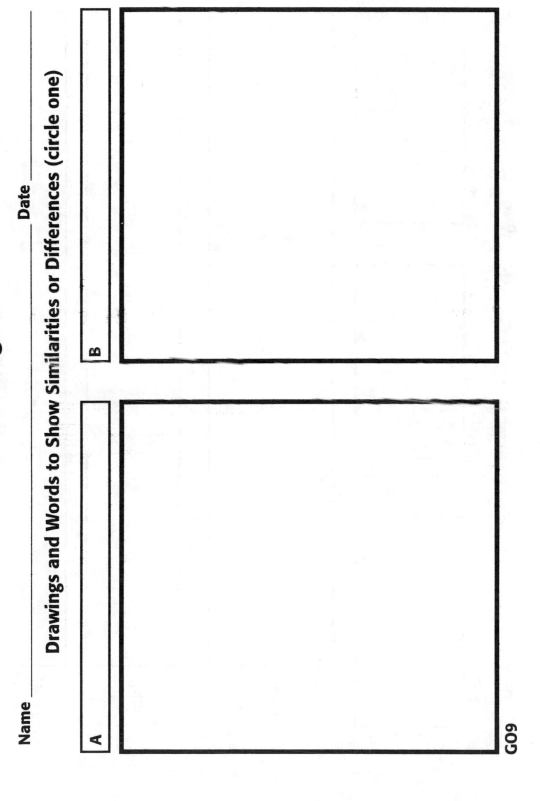

A

B

GO9

Name

Date:

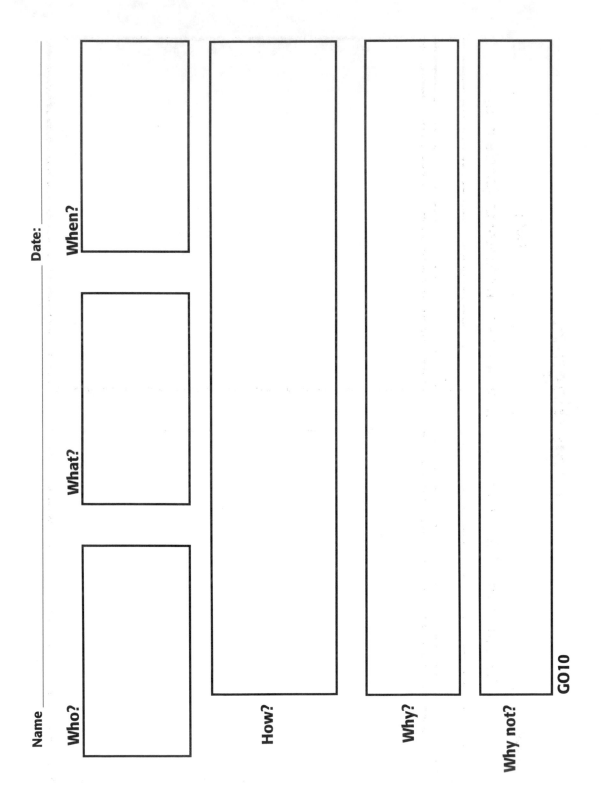

Who?

What?

When?

How?

Why?

Why not?

GO10

Four Boxes Of Details

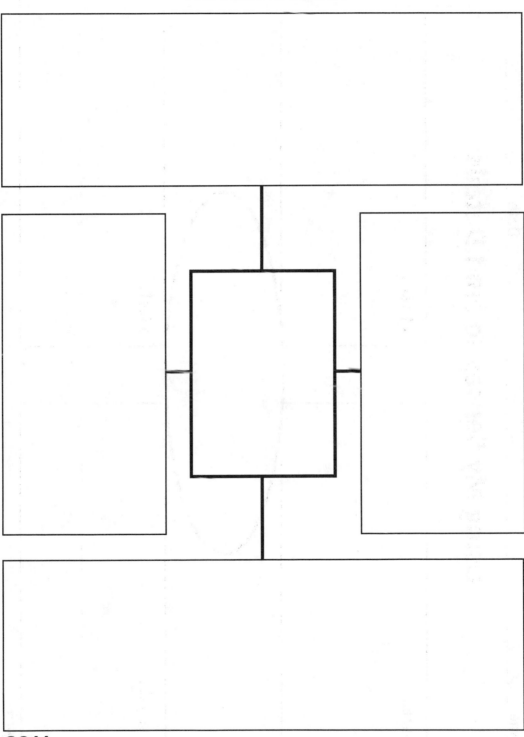

GO11

Name _____

Date _____

Using My Senses To Find Details

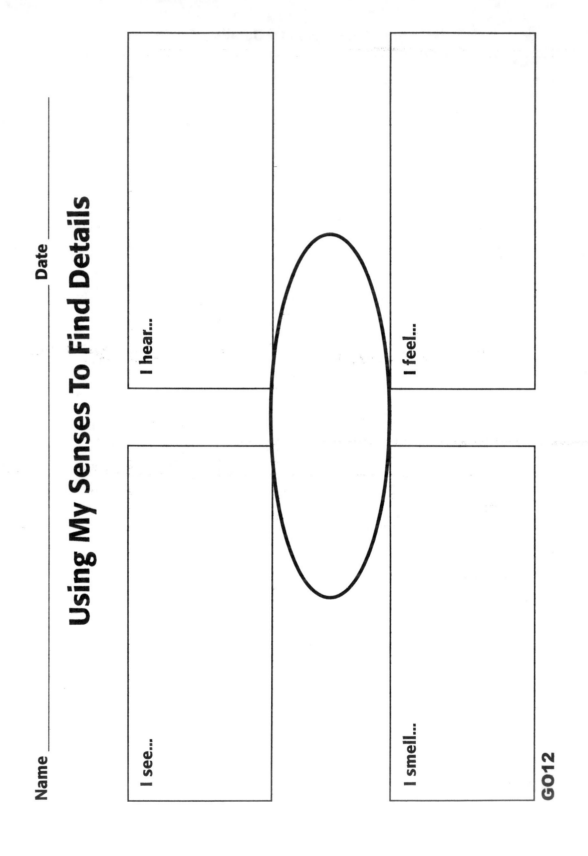

I see...

I hear...

I smell...

I feel...

GO12

Name: _____ **Date:** _____

Main Ideas and Details

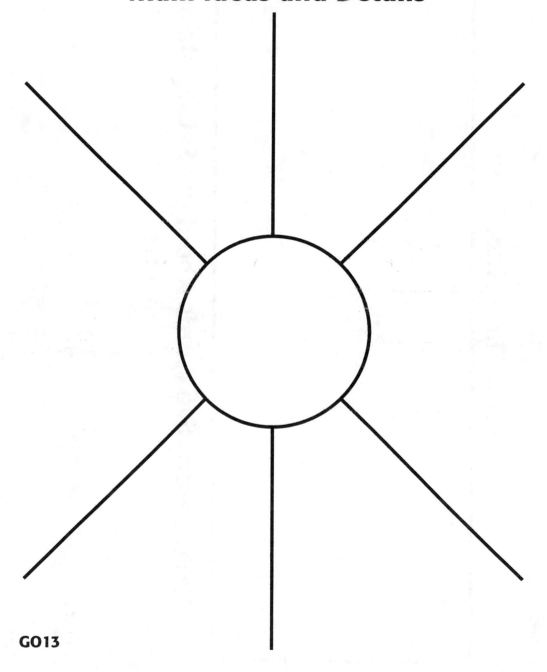

GO13

Name: _____ Dare: _____

Draw The Setting Here

Write Descriptive Words About the Setting Below

I see...

I smell...

I hear...

I feel...

GO14

Name: _____ Date: _____

Draw the Main Character Here

Write words that describe the character...

Size		Features

Clothing		Facial expression

GO15

Unusual characteristics

Performance Task Assessment List for Graphic Organizer GO15: Describe

Item	Assessment Points Possible	Points Earned — Assessed by Self	Points Earned — Assessed by Teacher
1. Did I draw the main character and show the character's size, clothing, facial expression, body features, and any unusual characteristics?	_____	_____	_____
2. Did I use color in a realistic way?	_____	_____	_____
3. Did I use proportion correctly?	_____	_____	_____
4. Is my drawing neat?	_____	_____	_____
5. Did I list words to describe the character's size, clothing, facial expression, body features, and any unusual characteristics?	_____	_____	_____
6. Is my spelling correct?	_____	_____	_____
Total	_____	_____	_____

Name: _____ Date: _____

Character: _____

Answer as if you were the character.

I am proud of _____

_____

_____

I am happy because _____

_____

_____

I am unhappy because _____

_____

_____

I am angry because _____

_____

_____

I am curious about _____

_____

_____

My strengths are _____

_____

_____

GO16 (2 pages)

My weakenesses are _____

_____

_____

I would describe myself as _____

_____

_____

Others would describe me as _____

_____

_____

I want to get better at _____

_____

_____

My goal in life is _____

_____

_____

Overall, the words that describe me are: _____

_____

_____

Name _____   Date _____

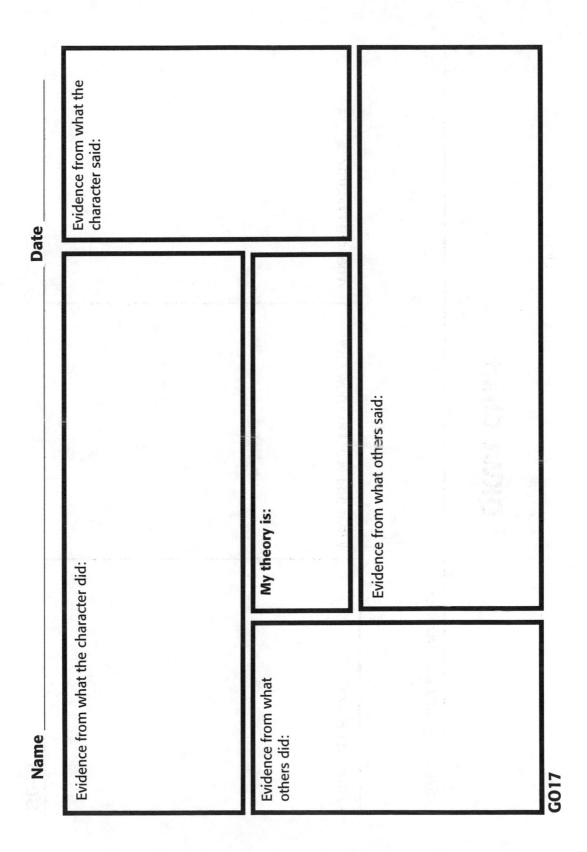

Evidence from what the character said:

Evidence from what the character did:

My theory is:

Evidence from what others did:

Evidence from what others said:

Name: _____   Date: _____

QKWL Chart

What is my research **Q**uestion?	
What do I **K**now?	What do I **W**ant to know?	What did I **L**earn?

Performance Task Assessment List for Graphic Organizer GO18: QKWL

	Item	Assessment Points Possible	Points Earned Assessed by Self	Assessed by Teacher
1.	Did I state my research question as a complete sentence?	____	____	____
2.	Is my research question on the correct topic?	____	____	____
3.	Did I list at least four things I already know about this topic?	____	____	____
4.	Did I list at least four things that I need to find out about this topic?	____	____	____
5.	Did I list at least four things that I learned through the research I did on this topic?	____	____	____
6.	Does my research answer my research question?	____	____	____
7.	Did I use complete sentences?	____	____	____
8.	Is my spelling correct?	____	____	____
9.	Is my work neat?	____	____	____
	Total	____	____	____

Name _____

Date _____

BookTitle _____

Reader's Rating For Fiction

0   **1**   **2**   **3**

I did not like
this book at all

I liked this
book a little.

I liked this
book a lot

This is my
favorite book.

I liked (or didn't like) this book because

_____

_____

_____

_____

_____

_____

_____

_____

GO19

Name _____ **Date** _____

The author (illustrator) did a good job of: _____

⬆ Yes	⬇ No

And this is why I think the way I do: _____

My Reasons	Support from the Text

Name: _____ Date: _____

Evaluating Information Sources

Title: _____

Author(s): _____

Date Published: _____

Check one box for each element used in this evaluation.
Add other elements if necessary.

Element	Rating			
	YES!!	Yes	No	NO!!
Can I read this material?				
Is this information about my topic?				
Is this information up-to-date?				
Is the author qualified to write on this topic?				
Do the illustrations and/or photographs give me good information?				
Comments				

GO21

Name: _____ **Date:** _____

Taking and Supporting a Position

Position:

Pros	Cons

Name _____

Date _____

BookTitle _____

Reader's Rating For Illustrations

0   **1**   **2**   **3**

I did not like the
illustrations at all.

I liked the
illustrations a little.

I liked the
illustrations a lot.

Wow! I loved
the illustrations!

I liked (or didn't like) the illustrations because

_____

_____

_____

_____

_____

_____

_____

_____

_____

GO23